DOUG M

THE RACE THAT CHANGED RUNNING

THE INSIDE STORY OF UTMB

The Race That Changed Running: The Inside Story of UTMB
By Doug Mayer

Photography: With photos from Howard Brundrett and other
photographers (see page 208 for photo credits)
Ultra-Trail®, Ultra-Trail du Mont-Blanc®, UTMB®, CCC®,
TDS® and PTL® are legally registered trademarks of UTMB
World Group and are used in this work with permission.
Cover Design Ewelina Proczko

ISBN: 978-3-039640-14-0

First Edition: June 2023
Printed in the Czech Republic

helvetiq.com

MIX
Paper from
responsible sources
FSC® C014138

THE RACE THAT
CHANGED
RUNNING

THE INSIDE STORY OF UTMB

BY DOUG MAYER

TABLE OF CONTENTS

DEDICATION

Dedicated to the path makers and maintainers of the Tour du Mont-Blanc, the unsung heroes of this story.

With gratitude to the dreamers and doers who created the world's most important trail race: René Bachelard, Jean-Claude Marmier, Catherine and Michel Poletti, Isabelle Poletti, Laurence Poletti-Gautier, Léon Lovey, Dédé Bozon and Mickaël Viseux.

"It is not the critic who counts; not the man who points out how the strong man stumbles, or where the doer of deeds could have done them better. The credit belongs to the man who is actually in the arena, whose face is marred by dust and sweat and blood; who strives valiantly; who errs, who comes short again and again, because there is no effort without error and shortcoming; but who does actually strive to do the deeds; who knows great enthusiasms, the great devotions; who spends himself in a worthy cause; who at the best knows in the end the triumph of high achievement, and who at the worst, if he fails, at least fails while daring greatly, so that his place shall never be with those cold and timid souls who neither know victory nor defeat".
– Theodore Roosevelt, Sorbonne, Paris, France, April 23, 1910

"Begin at the beginning, and go on till you come to the end: then stop."
- Lewis Carroll, Alice in Wonderland

KILIAN JORNET
"THE VALUES OF THE PEOPLE"

A year before my first UTMB, in 2008, a friend sent me a video of the race and I thought, "Oh, that looks fun!" It seemed really logical to run around Mont Blanc and I became interested. But I wondered—is it possible for me to run a hundred miles? That was the big question. I was nineteen and had run a marathon in the mountains and even longer hut-to-hut days alone, but I had never run a hundred miles. I knew if I could finish, I could win, but I didn't know if I would be able to finish.

To prepare I did the Tour du Mont-Blanc in four days and then in two days. After that I knew I could finish. When the time came to start, I was relaxed and excited about the adventure.

My plan was to run every step, even if slowly, and not to walk. I was with Dawa Sherpa for the first 20K or so, but then I ran alone for the rest of the race at a comfortable pace. It was a beautiful, still day—hot weather, a clear night. I felt pretty good. Of course, once I got to Switzerland it started to be painful, but that's normal.

UTMB 2022: "IT'S RACE MODE. LET'S RACE!"

I think UTMB 2022 was my 500th trail and ski-mountaineering race, not counting some small events. When I was young, UTMB was so big—it was everything to me. But now, I've learned not to get too excited at the start. Or stressed. It's just a race.

In 2022, from the beginning something was weird. Normally I'm good at downhills, but my coordination was off. I wondered what was going on. I started to feel really bad and could feel the Covid I'd had a few weeks before. By the end of the night, which is always the hardest moment, I was mentally out of the race. That's when Mathieu Blanchard passed me.

We talked for a minute and he said, "Oh Kilian, I'm sorry to pass you." I told him to go for his race. He was racing really well. I tried to forget everything and just stay with him. As I did, I felt myself completely change mentally. I went from feeling bad to, "It's race mode, let's race!"

We started to run together, caught Jim Walmsley, and then it was time to be smart and strategic. After Champex-Lac, I wanted to see how strong Mathieu was. I had never competed with him before, so I needed to understand him as a runner. We had two, maybe three uphills until the finish. I used the first uphill to study him. I pushed hard to see if he could follow or if he was losing time, if he was a pusher or more of a steady runner. Then, on the downhill, I knew I was not running well, so I wanted to see how much time he was able to recover.

After Vallorcine, I needed to make my move. I knew in the last downhill, from Flégère, Mathieu would make up five minutes easily and I needed to gain that time in the uphill. I knew I could sustain that uphill pace for some time, so I just tried to leave him. I did the work.

WE HAVE AN IMPACT. WE HAVE A RESPONSIBILITY.

As trail runners, we have an impact. So, therefore, we have a responsibility. This sport is not better or worse than the community around it. It is a reflection of who we are as humans.

When we talk about values in sport, the sport itself is immaterial. What we are talking about, really, are the values of the people. We need to accept that the sport is not "my sport" or "your sport." It's the community's sport, and the community is diverse.

PROTECTING THE UNIVERSAL VALUES OF TRAIL RUNNING

Trail running has some universal values. Respect for nature, fair play and helping each other all come before competition. The rest is up to the individual and whether you feel part of that particular community.

Trail running is now diverse. That's a good thing and one thing I hope will never be lost. You have UTMB, and you have Hardrock and Kima and Zegama. They have completely different ambiences and a lot of other differences, and that's a good thing for the sport. Of course, they also share those universal values like respect for nature.

Some sports just have one model, and everything is very much the same. Triathlon is like that—it's really just one thing: super tech, super pro. In trail running, we have different kinds of experiences, and I think that's great.

AN APPRECIATION FOR DIVERSITY

I think races have a responsibility to trail running. That's where the community needs the tools to have an impact. Now, that's not the case. Our only choice is to enter the race, or not.

It's important for there to be ways for the community to put external pressure on races, so that we can say, "Hey, you need to listen." Races need to share trail running's universal values. For example, if [the international gas company] Total sponsored a trail race, I'm not sure we'd agree that we share their set of values.

In my case, I'm able to talk with Michel Poletti about topics like antidoping, but that's only because we have a personal relationship. And these topics should not be linked to personal relationships.

I think people project the race they want to organize onto other races. But, you're not the organizer. If you want to organize a race, you can do it, and you can do it with your own values. If I were organizing a race, it would not be UTMB because it's not necessarily the values that are closest to me. However, I understand their model and I accept it. Of course, there are some aspects I don't like so much. But I appreciate the diversity.

DEFINING OUR COMMUNITIES' BOUNDARIES

As a community, we should define the boundaries that we should not cross. The trail running community needs a way to express itself as a group. I think it can be the role of federations to protect the values of a sport—to protect such things as fair play, and to develop the next generation of trail runners.

The problem is that for us, in trail running, the federations are kind of a mess. So, in our case, now, it falls to the community to do the work. We see that in the US, where volunteering is important. Or in the UK, for example, where the community has created races that are super accessible and just cost something like five pounds. In central Europe, we have a model that is more on the business side of things. There are volunteers, too, but there's also a lot of visibility and hype. Even if a lot of the work is done by the community, the brands have very high visibility.

I wouldn't say that I'm pro-federation. I would say instead that I'm pro open-source. I like the idea that the community creates the values, and it's up to the individual to take personal responsibility. That open-source approach works well in super small communities that are really well glued together. In those cases, nobody takes advantage of the situation.

The challenge comes when communities grow. If you want to grow something, you then start to look to protect yourself, and that sometimes means you will not listen to important parts of the community. And of course, sometimes, people take advantage of the situation. I think the challenge is how to build these links, even with a private organization, towards a better sport or a better race.

We're humans. It's not easy. It's complicated. This sport, it's not better or worse than society. The good news is that I think we agree on 90% of the values. The differences are not that big.

Kilian Jornet, January 2023

August 26, 2022: It had taken nineteen years to reach this point. For the race on this day, more than thirty thousand people had traveled from around the world to Chamonix, France. Many of them now lined the streets of the historic alpine town. Two thousand, six hundred twenty-seven runners had won coveted places at the start and were now packed tightly below the church. Huge screens broadcast their nervous faces. The crowd erupted in cheers as, one by one, some of the world's most decorated runners ran the first few hundred meters of the course in reverse, past thousands of spectators, to get to the elite starting zone at the front of the race.

A huge high-tech arch bearing the logos of sponsors towered over the start line in front of the mayor's office in Place du Triangle de l'Amitié. Some had paid into seven figures to be associated with this moment. Overhead, a helicopter filmed the race, one of many cameras feeding live coverage to the media center at Le Majestic Congress in Chamonix. Other cameras were carried on e-mountain bikes and in the arms of nimble rollerbladers. At the media center nearby, in an imposing Belle Epoque edifice that was once a grand hotel for adventurous Englishmen, a broadcast center fed a steady stream of the race to viewers in English, Spanish, French, Chinese, and Japanese. Over the course of the race, 25 million viewers would tune in to the live streams and highlight reels. Millions more would follow posts shared across a half dozen different platforms.

And those, for the most part, were just the people who loved UTMB. In Chamonix and around the world, there were also those who hated it. People who saw a race that was no longer about the running, directors who had sold out to multinational corporations, part of a "trail running-industrial complex" that was getting worse every year. More and more, there were voices crying out that far from making trail running what it is, UTMB had broken it.

At the center of it all, in the best position at the starting line, was the American Katie Schide, one of the world's fastest and strongest ultrarunners. And this year, she was going for it. In her eyes, she had nothing to lose.

What had happened? How had a simple idea—to run a race around the highest mountain in the Alps—become this, not only the most important trail race in the world, but a mega event, deserving to be mentioned in the same league as the America's Cup sailing race or Ironman Hawaii or even the Tour de France itself. How had it, in the process, influenced runners around the world, and taken the niche sport of trail running into the mainstream?

Katie Schide went out fast, sprinting past the thousands of roaring fans. "I felt good, really good," Katie later told me. Would the speed up front hurt later? Schide didn't care. "I've been there. I know what the bottom feels like," she said. "I figured, 'I can deal with that when the time comes.'" Besides, she thought, the other times she had done UTMB it had not gone according to plan, even though she had landed in eighth and sixth place. So why be conservative?

In addition to Schide, a small pack of men pushed the pace. They were the world's best trail runners, including two who were widely considered the favorites. US runner Jim Walmsley had moved to Arêches-Beaufort, near Chamonix, earlier in the year, expressly to train for UTMB. But the most famous of the men at the starting line that day was the Catalan runner Kilian Jornet, indisputably the best trail runner of his generation. Jornet had come to the starting line with little pomp; he wore a surgical mask because, several weeks earlier, he had contracted COVID-19.

"UTMB is a transformative experience," said Topher Gaylord, one of the most longstanding observers of UTMB. "You put yourself in Chamonix and have the opportunity to run through three countries and around the rooftop of Europe, and experience all the emotions of life in a single day. UTMB delivers you back to Chamonix a changed human being."

STATIC IN A SUPERCHARGED WORLD

Like others from my generation, I had started trail running as a supplement to outdoor sports like climbing and backcountry skiing. I enjoyed pushing hard in New Hampshire's White Mountains, the rugged and technical range outside my backdoor in the mountain town of Randolph, population 310. For a decade, my interest slowly grew, and I enjoyed tackling big days and long nights of forty or fifty miles through challenging terrain. Through relatives, I had access to an aging but cozy chalet in the Alps. There, I explored new trails in Switzerland's French-speaking Valais. I started to race, running double vertical-kilometers and hundred-mile events, landing in the top 20% on a good day. Through trial and error, I learned to manage my body and mind. I became, in short, an ultrarunner.

For many of those years, though many European trail runners were obsessed with UTMB, I didn't pay it much attention. I ran smaller, community-based races around the Alps and enjoyed exploring less-traveled trails. In 2015, however, I started spending summers in Chamonix, drawn to one of the world's trail running hubs for my new tour company, Run the Alps. In 2017, I moved to the valley year-round. I started writing about the lively trail running scene there, and gradually was pulled into the UTMB orbit.

The more I wrote about the race, the more questions I had. Everyone, it seemed, had a strong opinion about the race, but few had a clear grip on anything more than the surface facts. Endless speculation seemed to be a part-time hobby for some Chamonix trail runners. Some told me the owners of the race were fabulously wealthy; others said the race was fundamentally a small business that pulled off a dramatic show for a week each year. I heard that the race organizers were, well, just about everything: passionate and dispassionate, open-minded and close-minded, inclusive and exclusive, tight-lipped and disarmingly frank, flexible and unyielding.

Over the years, as the race grew, I would sit down with Catherine or Michel Poletti, the couple who were the two central founders of the race and its driving force, and we would talk—usually for an interview for *Trail Runner Magazine*, where I was a contributing editor. And each time, I was

surprised by what I learned. UTMB, I began to realize, was both the most important race in trail running and the least well understood.

Whatever you think of UTMB—and the opinions run the gamut—the race matters. And if you care about trail running, you need to care about what happens at UTMB. And yet there was so much static. What I wanted most—an honest, unvarnished look at the UTMB story—didn't exist.

I had also experienced the many sides of UTMB firsthand. When Run the Alps was little more than a homemade website and a somewhat ridiculous sounding idea, I received a stack of papers from a Paris law firm, insisting I cease and desist from using the trademarked name of the race in a few mentions on the *Run the Alps* website. Coincidentally, I had spent years at National Public Radio enforcing the trademark for its most popular show, *Car Talk,* for which I was a producer. I was stunned by the heavy-handed opening volley, which was not my style. I imagined myself involved in a transcontinental lawsuit. I quickly removed the few passing references. (Only during the course of writing this book did I find out that UTMB was then doing battle with a whole slew of brands that were intentionally leveraging the race's name for profit, while UTMB partners were asking, "Why bother paying a licensing fee for your name when everyone else just uses it for free?")

Years later, I saw a different side of the organization. Running UTMB's 119-kilometer TDS race, I spotted Michel Poletti in the far corner of the aid station at Lac Combal, not far from Courmayeur, Italy, assisting race volunteers. I had assumed he would be flying over the race in a helicopter or offering commentary in front of a TV camera. He was an important figure, after all. And UTMB was very, very big.

"Michel," I said, "What are you doing here?"

"I'm exactly where I want to be," he said, smiling. In other words: out of the limelight, supporting the volunteers, encouraging the runners. Being the heart and soul of the trail-running community.

My own trail running in the Alps continued to develop, as did my company. I ran the big-name races, vertiginous skyraces that required a climbing helmet, and dozens of local events where the question was always the same. "Vous êtes américain? Comment avez-vous découvert cette course?" ("You're American? How did you find out about this race?") Entirely for fun and by accident, I learned more and more about the scene.

After some years and many interviews, and after running four of the UTMB races myself (and three of them twice), I realized I was in an intriguing and unique position—what I called my Forrest Gump world—a gauzy, dreamy scene into which I had stumbled like Alice in Wonderland. I was now a Chamonix local, but with American trail-running DNA. I was a trail runner and a writer, with one foot in the mountains and the other in the trail-running business. I was, in short, in a unique position to tell the UTMB story. I had come to see both the organization and its staff and owners from many angles and in all their complexity.

What I discovered intrigued me: a largely unknown history that was rich and authentic. An organization that seemed mighty and all-powerful from the outside but felt like a small business with growing pains on the inside. There were curious announcements that seemed incomprehensible to my American mind but had their own rationale behind them. (Even if I sometimes still strongly disagreed with the choices made.)

UTMB is, above all, a very human story, and I have had the good fortune to sit in a front-row seat, taking it all in.

My goal is simple: to tell the story honestly.

Let me now try to take you there.

The Ultra-Trail du Mont-Blanc has taken its place as one of the world's great sporting events. It has influenced runners around the world and has helped bring the niche sport of trail running into the mainstream.

It was not, however destined to do so. In fact, that there is a trail race around Mont Blanc at all can be traced back to one spry ninety-year-old gentleman who was wandering among the packed crowd on August 28, 2022, but went entirely unnoticed: René Bachelard.

A MEETING IN THE STREETS OF CHAMONIX

René Bachelard had a distinguished military career in which he rose to become a general in the French Army. Following his mandatory retirement from the army at age 57, he oversaw construction projects in and around Lyon, France. He and his wife moved to her childhood home of Chamonix, where the family had been coming for summer vacations. While not an elite athlete, Bachelard enjoyed hiking, skiing, and—more recently—trail running. In 1998, he was elected president of the Chamonix Mont Blanc Marathon, or CMBM. It was a position he would hold for nearly twenty years. (The CMBM name, inspired by the idea of running marathon distances, actually pre-dates and is not associated with the Marathon du Mont-Blanc.)

In the fall of 2002, however, Bachelard was annoyed by a decision by CMBM's parent organization, Chamonix's Club des Sports, the town's lively running club, to cancel that fall's relay race around Mont Blanc.

In 1999, a major fire in the Mont Blanc tunnel connecting Chamonix with Courmayeur had brought the Club des Sports' Tour du Mont-Blanc seven-person relay race to a halt. Life had continued in the two mountain towns, but an important link between them had been severed, and coordination became time-consuming and challenging. Investigations were undertaken, and extensive repairs were needed. For three years, the tunnel remained closed.

Now that it had reopened, suddenly, the race could happen—but lackluster promotion had led to only a small number of registrations. Whenever Bachelard crossed paths with Michel Poletti, a local runner also in CMBM, he expressed his anger. "Again and again, it was the same thing," remembers Poletti. "'We need to do something! We need to relaunch the race around Mont Blanc.'"

Bachelard had fond memories of the seven-runner relay race around the peak that loomed above Chamonix and viewed it as a powerful symbol uniting France, Italy, and Switzerland. He remembers those encounters, too. "I was a big pain in the ass because I kept asking everyone, 'Can we

Trient

Champex-Lac

Vallorcine

La Tête Aux Vents

La Fouly

Switzerland

Chamonix

France

Italy

Grand Col Ferret

Saint-Gervais-les-Bains

Arnouvaz

Mont Blanc

Les Contamines

Courmayeur

Lac Combal

Col de la Seigne

Les Chapieux

do a race around Mont Blanc?' I was bugging everyone!" In Michel Poletti, Bachelard found someone who would listen.

In many ways, Bachelard was an unlikely advocate. His longest previous run had been the town's 23-kilometer Cross du Mont-Blanc—which he ran despite having once watched it and sworn that he would never run even that comparatively short distance. "I saw the finish of the Cross and I said 'I would never do that!' I had run 21 kilometers before, but there was all of that up and down!"

For years, Michel Poletti had been curious about the possibility of a continuous run around Mont Blanc and was eager to try it himself. He dug through dusty archives in Chamonix, researching the history of prior attempts. There were some interesting hints that such a race might be feasible. Poletti uncovered the story of Chamonix locals Jacky Duc and Christian Roussel, who in 1978 ran around Mont Blanc in 24 hours and 45 minutes. During that period, Duc was the caretaker of the Refuge du Plan de l'Aiguille, a mountain hut high above Chamonix. He went on to run the loop solo a year later in 21 hours, 40 minutes, according to journalist Julien Gilleron. Edith Coue became the first woman confirmed to have run around Mont Blanc, ticking off the loop in 28:02:30 in 1980. In 1995, Poletti tried it himself. Pushing around the mountain partly with friends and partly alone, he ultimately called it quits in Ferret, Switzerland. "You can understand," he told me, "what it meant to me to be part of organizing this race. From the first moment, I had said, 'I'm running it!'"

There had already been running races around the 4,807-meter-high Mont Blanc, the highest peak in Western Europe. For three years, starting in 1987, the Mont-Blanc Maratour was run as a four-stage race. Later came the Super Marathon du Mont-Blanc, a three-stage race that included significant sections on roads to speed up the resulting times. Poorly organized and hampered by bad weather during several editions, it peaked at just eighty runners. Last on the list was the Tour du Mont-Blanc Ultra Marathon, organized by Chamonix's Club des Sports and its running division, the CMBM. There were seven editions of this seven-person relay in various formats, but the event still focused largely on speed and elite athletes.

Now, the tunnel was reopened, but no race was happening. And with trail running in ascendance, some thought the Club des Sports was tone-deaf. "There's too much tar, and not enough spirit of the trail," said Michel Poletti at the time of the announcement of the race's cancellation in 2002.

Bachelard was relentless. His pestering continued, and Poletti agreed to call a meeting. At it, an intriguing topic was debated: would it be a relay race as in past years, or could the loop be done by each runner in one epic push? Poletti and others advocated for a continuous 100-mile race around Mont Blanc. It wasn't entirely unreasonable, as recent ultra-distance trail races had proven.

It was time for a new idea. But no race had ever existed quite like what Michel Poletti wanted to try. His idea was bold—one epic push around the enormous massif at the meeting point of Italy, France, and Switzerland.

THE MONT BLANC MASSIF

Before the first mountain races, before the trail that connected the three countries, and before even the countries themselves, there was the mountain.

And before the mountain—hundreds of millions of years before—there was a sea. It was later named for the sea goddess Tethys, who nourished the earth with her six thousand children, themselves rivers and streams and rain clouds. The massive marine reptile ichthyosaur, one of the largest animals ever to roam the planet, swam in her waters. Some ichthyosaurs were 65 feet long. Other dinosaurs walked along the shoreline; their footprints are still visible today within sight of Mont Blanc.

Imperceptibly and over millions of years, sediment from the remains of the teeming ocean life collected along the seafloor. Deep under the sediment was liquid magma, which cooled into the minerals feldspar, quartz, and mica, eventually morphing into granite a dozen or so kilometers under the sea. Over the course of forty million years, this plate of rock collided with an African plate to the south. Where they met, the two plates pushed skyward, creating an enormous swath of gigantic wrinkles across thousands of square kilometers of the planet.

Thus were born the Alps.

Over this new, rocky surface, entire ecosystems came and went at the mercy of the earth's temperature. Glaciers crept forward and retreated like an icy wave lapping over the continent. During the retreats, lichens and mosses were followed by grasses, flowers, shrubs, and finally trees.

The Mont Blanc region of the Alps is huge, encompassing 400 square kilometers over parts of Italy, France, and Switzerland. Within the massif today, there are 159 square kilometers of glaciers and eleven summits over 4,000 meters.

During the most recent ice age, early humans arrived from Africa. Ten thousand years ago, they gathered in the valleys of the Alps, living off deer and chamois on land and fish from the rivers. When they began herding animals, they moved to higher pastures with them in the summers, initiating the annual Alpine rhythm called transhumance that persists to this day.

Cultures developed in the Alpine valleys. The dominant Celts extended their sway throughout the Alps and much of Europe. At the periphery, cultures collided, leading to wars. There was little respite from the bloodshed: first came the Roman Empire, then Venice's oversight, the Houses of Savoy, Visconti, and Hapsburg, and finally the arrival of Napoleon in 1798. Small duchies merged, and in time the modern countries of France, Italy, and Switzerland began to take shape.

In the summers, irrespective of who was governing, herders watched over their animals in the high Alps, and trails formed between the villages and the summer pastures. Some of these trails developed into trade routes.

Aristocracy merged with mountaineering in the person of the Swiss geologist Horace Benedict de Saussure. In 1767, laden with scientific instruments, he completed a circumnavigation of Mont Blanc, likely becoming the first person to knowingly loop the mountain: undoubtedly an ultra, of a kind.

Two decades later and a year after the first ascent of Mont Blanc—which Saussure inspired with a cash reward—he became the third person to reach the summit. The moment is legendary, enshrined in mountaineering history as the genesis of modern alpinism. Saussure's explorations and subsequent writings set in motion a golden age of tourism that spread from Europe's aristocrats to the less well-heeled.

More than a century later, in 1924, Chamonix hosted the first Winter Olympics, cementing its position as a worldwide hub of outdoor sports.

Two world wars ravaged the Alps and their inhabitants. There were battles around the mountain, including along the Tour du Mont-Blanc, most notably at Col de la Seigne on the French–Italian border. In the Battle of the Alps, on June 21, 1940, the Italians took control of the Col. Three days later, they stormed Cormet de Roselend, where today UTMB's TDS race has a large aid station. France signed armistice agreements with Italy and Germany later that day, and the fighting ceased—though a final Battle of the Alps took place on the south side of Mont Blanc in spring, 1945. It would be Italy's last battle of World War II. Today, runners and hikers with a careful eye can spot the aging fortifications.

Airplanes became more common in the skies above the glaciers of Mont Blanc. High above the course of the UTMB, not too far from Col de la Seigne, a US B-17 Flying Fortress bomber crashed in the early morning hours of November 1, 1946. Eight aviators died. The impact was so great that the plane disintegrated completely, spreading debris into two countries.

The mountain and the intertwined trails around its base entered our modern era. Communities worked on the ancient paths, upgrading them for tourists who sought them out. In the 1960s, old huts were updated to meet the needs of a new generation of mountain climbers. Inns sprung up in the valleys, and on July 19, 1965, the tunnel connecting Chamonix with Courmayeur was inaugurated. It saved two hours of travel time and became a key corridor through the Alps.

And so, long before the arrival of Gore-Tex clad trail runners and their own individual tales of personal challenge, the mountain was already steeped in legend and rich with human history.

Bachelard and the locals on the new committee knew much of this history, and it was partly what drew them to create their own stories here.

UNABLE TO EAT FOR MILES

Katie Schide, in her own way, was now part of the story. Twenty years after Bachelard convinced Michel Poletti to help make his dream come true, on a beautiful day in August 2022, Schide was pushing herself hard. She stayed in front for over a dozen hours, but the dreaded crash finally came—and hard. Unable to eat for miles, her body rebelled at Arnouvaz, Italy, 98 kilometers into the race. Just outside the aid station, where she had chugged a Coke in search of quick calories, she vomited. During the 780-meter climb to Grand Col Ferret on the Swiss-Italian border, Canadian runner Marianne Hogan flew past. "She passed me like I was standing still," Schide remembered. "I thought, 'Well, that's it. I'll just let her go. I'm still near the front of the race.'" Schide knew they were both on record pace. Was it sustainable? "Maybe Marianne's having the race of her life," she remembers thinking. There was no catching her. Or was there?

Just a few hours later, a not dissimilar drama would play out in the same location. Through much of the early night, the men's lead pack coalesced into four runners: Jornet, Walmsley, UK runner Tom Evans and US runner Zach Miller. Ten minutes behind the four, hanging back, was French runner Mathieu Blanchard. "At Col du Bonhomme," Walmsley told me, "you start to see who is really putting their hat into the ring." But by the time the group reached the big aid station at the Courmayeur Sports Center, it was down to two: Walmsley and Jornet.

Between Courmayeur, Italy, and La Fouly, Switzerland, Walmsley opened a solid fourteen-minute lead. But the effort cost him. One hundred thirty kilometers in, on the 770-meter climb to the high Swiss pasture known as Bovine, he crashed hard. First Jornet passed, then Blanchard. By the time they left the aid station in Trient, Jornet and Blanchard were leading Walmsley by 19 minutes. "In my mind, when I left Trient, I thought I was going to catch back up," he told *Trail Runner Magazine*. "I've gotten to Trient before and been able to rebound on the way to Chamonix. I was thinking I'd be able to harness that again," Walmsley told me. "But immediately when I hit the hill, I thought, 'No way.' I was so shot. The hill out of Trient was very much a reality check that I was deep under water." In the last 50 km back to Chamonix, Walmsley grew reflective. "The final three hours felt like a year. I got to think a lot. The race I was hoping for didn't happen. I thought about what I can do to prepare for next year, and not to repeat the same mistakes." Walmsley would go on to finish fourth, after Tom Evans. What happened to Jornet and Blanchard is the stuff of legend (see Chapter 3).

Heroic dramas unfold on the UTMB course. It seemed that what had happened to Walmsley was about to happen to Katie Schide.

But if she was out of energy, Schide was not out of ideas. She remembered how a friend, Camille Bruyas, had eaten a cheese sandwich in La Fouly, regained her strength, and gone on to finish second in the women's race the year before. Schide thought, "Why not?" And after a cheese sandwich, she found new life. A twenty-minute gap closed to minutes and then, finally, Schide passed Hogan. Woozy but still pushing hard, she remembers thinking, "Okay... I passed the girl who was first. That must mean... I'm in first." There was nothing else in her mind. "I was kind of blacked out," she said. She does remember her coach, Jason Koop, telling her at the Trient aid station, "All you need to do is take care of yourself." It was not such a small ask. There were still many kilometers and two big climbs to go.

UTMB BY THE NUMBERS

RACE COURSE STATS

ELEVATION GAIN
9,963 meters/32,687 feet (2022)

DISTANCE
171 kilometers/106 miles (2022)

NUMBER OF KEY CLIMBS
10

NUMBER OF RUNNERS
2626 (2022)

TIME CUT OFF
46:30

RECORD FINISH TIME
Courtney Dauwalter 22 hours 30 minutes (2021)
Kilian Jornet 19 hours 49 minutes (2022)

PERCENTAGE OF WOMEN RUNNERS
9.3% (2022)

HIGHEST POINT (COL DES PYRAMIDES CALCAIRES)
2,567 meters/8,422 feet

LOWEST POINT (SAINT-GERVAIS, FRANCE)
826 meters/2,710 feet

UTMB LIVE VIEWERSHIP
100M minutes of videos viewed (2022)

UTMB THEN AND NOW

PRIZE MONEY (AWARDED TO BOTH TOP MEN AND TOP WOMEN FINISHERS)
2003: €0
2022: 1st €10,000
      2nd €5000
      3rd €3000
      4th, 5th €1500
      6th–10th €1000

COMPLETION RATE BY YEAR
2004: 30%
2022: 68.2%

NUMBER OF NATIONALITIES AT THE STARTING LINE
2003: 19
2022: 75

GOING LONG IN THE MOUNTAINS

By the time Katie Schide arrived in France, UTMB was so well established it was hard to comprehend how very uncertain it all was for the organizing committee back in 2002.

Of course, trail running in the Alps was nothing new. Long ago, it was just called "running." One history of Chamonix recounts a race to the summit of the Brévent in the Aiguilles Rouges, north of town. It was held August 8th, 1897. Ten guides from the Compagnie des Guides took part. Foreshadowing a race that would come 106 years and a few weeks later, it too started and finished on the steps of the St. Michel Church. Edouard Payot ticked off the route in two hours, a time that is quite fast even by today's standards. He received 100 francs for his effort.

Mountain running races came into their own in the Alps in the 1970s, with events like Dents-du-Midi and Sierre-Zinal in Switzerland, and the Cross du Mont-Blanc and Nid d'Aigle in France. These races were generally short, fast, and highly competitive.

In the decade before UTMB arrived, longer races in the mountains were just beginning to appear in France. The new sport, called trail running, owed much to the United States. In 1989, sports journalists Gilles Bertrand and Odile Baudrier covered two trail ultras in the US, a 100-mile long race in Leadville, Colorado, and the 100-mile long Western States Endurance Run in California. Captivated by what they saw, they launched the 65-kilometer Grande Course des Templiers in 1995. (Templiers continues to this day and has now burgeoned to a dozen races.)

Michel Poletti would discover these longer runs on mountain trails in 2000, after returning from an April trip to Norway having finished the longest cross-country ski race he had ever done—95 kilometers. It took him eight hours. "It was tough, but it was good," he told me. Afterward, he wanted to know...could he go longer?

It was good timing. "Grand Raid" trail races were cropping up around France—in the Mercantour in the south, and even on France's Reunion Island in the Indian Ocean. These races mixed hiking with running and covered vast distances.

Poletti's ultra career did not get off to an auspicious start, however. Just two months after the trip to Norway, he started a 140-kilometer race in the Pyrenees, the Grand Raid Ariège. It was halted mid-race due to severe weather. La Fort'iche de Maurienne was next, 120 kilometers long with 7,000 meters of climbing. But there, he went off course, crossing the border into Italy. By the time he figured out his error, another storm had moved in, forcing runners to stop. (Poletti returned twice and finally ticked off the full course.)

Poletti and three others in CMBM were increasingly pulled into this new sport. The spirit seemed different from mountain running. With its sense of adventure, trail running promoted self-sufficiency and had a vibe that was less about competition and more about personal discovery and inclusiveness—about finishing rather than winning. These races, some of which lasted dozens of hours, were fundamentally different from earlier ones. Poletti would finally race Templiers in 2002.

Even though a few long-distance trail races had started to appear, the idea of a 100-mile race around Western Europe's highest point was daring. The logistics alone were daunting. There were differing regulations in Switzerland, France, and Italy. There was the question of communications around the Mont-Blanc massif. Each town around the mountain would have to issue permission. Volunteers and medical professionals who spoke English plus one of the two local languages were needed along the course. And there was the trail itself. Some of the modern-day Tour du Mont-Blanc route, such as the section between Rifugio Bertone and Refugio Bonatti above Courmayeur, had not even been built.

And always there was the issue of the weather. The Mont Blanc massif has "big mountain" weather, and conditions can switch from summer to winter in minutes. Blizzard-like conditions are a possibility in every month of the year. The haunting question, "What if someone dies?", remained unasked. And it was not theoretical. Fifteen years earlier, on October 9, 1987, forty runners had taken part in the first edition of the three-day Super Marathon du Mont-Blanc stage race. On the first day of the race, at Col de la Seigne on the French–Italian border, a runner perished from exposure.

It soon became apparent that the daunting run itself was only part of the challenge. The race needed more than just eager runners. It needed race directors who could launch an event of mind-boggling complexity. It needed Catherine and Michel Poletti, forty-nine and forty-seven respectively, who, between them, combined skills as unlikely as piano playing, paragliding, and event organizing, and who had once, years before, owned Chamonix's most popular record store.

LOVE AT FIRST STRIKE

Catherine Causse and Michel Poletti met during a student strike at the University of Grenoble at the edge of the French Alps. In the spring of 1974, echoes of France's student rebellion of May 1968 were still reverberating on campuses around the country. Causse and Poletti, both progressive idealists working towards advanced degrees, eagerly took part. Michel's university was striking to protest reforms proposed by the French Minister of Education Alice Saunier-Seité, and Catherine joined the cause, making pancakes to raise money to support the strikers. "We were going to Paris to start the revolution," she told me. "It was," she noted, "perhaps the first time we each realized we loved organizing events. It was peace and love, and all that." "It was beautiful," adds Michel. "But in the end, some of it was perhaps not so realistic."

Michel Poletti, born and raised in the mountain culture of Chamonix, was intrigued by the sensibilities of the young Catherine Causse, who had grown up in an academic and artistic household. Her father taught at écoles d'agriculture—agricultural schools—around France, and even in Morocco for four years. The family home was filled with music: two brothers played violin, a sister played flute, Catherine's mother played the

↑ *CATHERINE AT GINKOIA, THE IT COMPANY CREATED BY THE POLETTIS* ↓ *CATHERINE 2002 WITH RELATIVES*

cello and her father played oboe and sang as a tenor. After school, there were painting, drawing, and classical dance classes for the young Causse daughter. Catherine spent her summers at music camps and trained to become a concert pianist. "Here was a representative from a new world, one very different from mine," Michel Poletti said. "She talked about music and art. I was really attracted to it."

For her part, Catherine immediately took to Poletti. "I had a deep sense of trust in him. I used a different form of logic, but it was logic all the same. Sometimes, it's impossible to explain the spark."

The two married in 1977. Michel was involved in the nascent world of computer science, studying early versions of computerized language translation. Catherine was studying psychology. In 1979—sooner than anticipated, Catherine observes—daughter Isabelle arrived. Catherine took on a full-time job to support the family, and Michel continued work on his degree.

The young family was on a track leading directly to a career in Paris, and as the path ahead became increasingly clear, Michel Poletti grew despondent. "It was the wrong way for me," he said. In his future he saw rush hours, long days in the city, and none of the Alps that he so loved. Catherine took counsel with a psychologist friend. "She told me, 'You have two choices. Move to Paris and take antidepressants, or go to Chamonix.'"

CHAMONIX-BOUND

A return to Chamonix in the works, the couple still had no idea where to live or how to make a living. They renovated a garage owned by Michel's father's masonry business in the south end of town, turning it into a chalet. The former garage of Entreprise Poletti off Rue du Lyret is still their home. "We didn't have enough money to buy a house in Chamonix. That would have been impossible for us," Michel told me. The living room's sunken floor, which to a visitor seems an intentional and stylish touch, was once the pit under which workers maintained the company vehicles. In those days, a vacant field opened up the view to the south. The location is unspectacular, tucked into a side street between the trendy four-star Heliopic Hotel and the D1506 thoroughfare that runs the length of the Chamonix valley. Inside, the home is warm and inviting. A variety of instruments hang on the walls, and there is an upright piano in one corner. Small sculptures adorn the interior, among them some UTMB finisher awards, sculpted by local climber and artist Andy Parkin.

There was still the question of how to make a living. Counseling in Chamonix would not have generated enough income to support a family. For Michel, teaching skiing or mountain guiding seemed appealing but required too many years of training. They needed steady cash. So, in December 1979, at 217 Avenue du Midi, trading on their shared passion for music, they opened a record shop.

Violni Records ran smoothly for some years, powered by the Polettis' love of everything from rap to classical. As the shop offered a wide range of music, the couple became knowledgeable about everything from AC/DC to Bach. "There is great music in every genre," Catherine told me. The two quickly ticked off a few of their favorites: Mozart. The Rolling Stones. The Doors. Led Zeppelin. ZZ Top. AC/DC. "Jazz, soul, classical, rock, world music—there's plenty to like," said Michel.

But their income was modest at best. The shop evolved to include a VHS movie club, offer some of the first home computer games, and even sell first-generation business computers. In 1987, Michel and Catherine became partners in a Grenoble company that developed retail inventory-management software. The new company, Algol, showed promise.

It was a busy decade for the couple, who steadily established themselves as part of the Chamonix business and social community. Michel's parents—who lived barely 80 meters away—helped care for Isabelle and then her brother, David, who arrived in 1987.

One day during the summer of 1986, quite literally out of the blue, a pilot with a steerable parachute contraption flew over their home and landed in the field next door. It was the first paraglider the Polettis had seen; in the days to come, they would see many more.

Michel became curious about the new sport and soon became a licensed pilot. Catherine joined a few years later, and together they would launch from Planpraz, 1,000 meters above town, and land conveniently right next to their house. They hung out with the paragliding crowd at La Calobée, just below the lift to Planpraz. Conversations sparked an idea, and in 1987, together with four friends, they organized an international paragliding competition.

"For me," said Catherine, "Paragliding was crazy! I loved to fly, but at the same time, when I was in the air, all I was thinking was, 'I need to land!'"

The Polettis' adventures with paragliding came to a dramatic head in September 1987, one week after David's birth. Elated by the new addition to the family, Michel celebrated by hopping on the first stage of the Aiguille du Midi cable car up to Plan de l'Aiguille, high above town. The weather was not ideal for parasailing, however. Winds were strong and buffeted the pilots. "I made the decision to fly, and it was a mistake," said Michel. He crashed during takeoff.

And so—just days after Catherine returned home from the old Chamonix hospital on Rue Vallot—Michel was admitted to the same hospital with compression fractures of several vertebrae and other injuries. He stayed a week. "My mother came to see her new grandson," said Catherine, "and I handed him to her and left, because there was no one else to open the record shop." Later that day, David returned to the hospital in the arms of his grandmother to see his father.

Michel continued to paraglide—more carefully now—and the competition was held again in 1988.

But something about the new sport didn't sit well with Catherine and Michel Poletti.

"The spirit of paragliding was always about doing something more and more difficult—the more dangerous your flight was, the better," said Michel. "It was the spirit of going to war and coming back as a survivor."

"Everyone needed to be a hero," Catherine said. "It was not what we

loved. It was all quite artificial. You always had to talk about how difficult your flight was." The Polettis found the braggadocio off-putting. "The stronger fliers had no respect for the beginners," said Catherine. It was a lesson that would inform much of how they would structure UTMB, celebrating anyone brave enough to come to the start line.

And then there were fatalities. When I spoke to Michel and Catherine about it, sitting together around the small kitchen table in their chalet, Catherine's usual matter-of-fact style showed a hint of breaking down.

"We lost many friends," she admitted.

Michel ticked through a list. "Jean Marc Boivin... Didier Escoffier... Bruno Gouvi."

"Too many friends died," Catherine confirmed, remembering what had happened decades ago. In their minds, sponsoring brands very clearly played a role in the fatalities. "The companies," said Catherine, "were pushing their athletes to do more and more." The sport, it seemed, was becoming filled with ghosts.

It was a pivotal moment for the Polettis, and in a sense, it set them up for what was to come next. "I realized I loved extreme sports, but more on the endurance side," said Michel.

For her part, Catherine was relieved that their flying days were over. "It was great for me when he decided to stop. We had two kids, a store, and an IT company. We were busy enough."

Catherine began to have problems with her hip, which would later require surgery. There were other, more mundane issues too, and the third edition of the international paragliding event didn't come to pass. "We discovered it was very difficult to run a large sports event as a non-profit organization. It made it harder to get a sponsor," said Catherine. "We knew that if we were going to organize an event again, it would have to be as a professional company." "If you want to do something perfectly," added Michel, "you need to do it professionally."

By the time Bachelard began pestering Michel, the couple had sold the record shop. Violni had become the victim of global trends that brought the demise of mom-and-pop record stores around the world. "During the 80s," said Michel, "it was becoming obvious that record stores in France were going to collapse."

Catherine was ready for a new project, and this new event seemed perfect. By 2002, the couple had accrued many of the skills necessary not only for creating a successful event but also for shepherding it through uncertain early years. And they had confidence—enough to plunge head-long into organizing a trail race through three countries and around one of the largest massifs in Europe.

And so, in September 2002, after persistent nudging from Bachelard, a group of nine trail runners met at the Hotel Faucigny in Chamonix. They boasted a wide variety of skills with a common thread: a love for the new-ly developing world of long-distance trail running. Their goal was clear, even if some in town thought it was downright foolish: to organize a trail race around Mont Blanc—and not run in stages or as a relay, but in one continuous effort.

The most recent race around Mont Blanc had been organized by the town's Club des Sports, and that made things easier. The committee now reached out to the key communities around the Mont-Blanc massif. The layers of bureaucracy and the process of trail selection sometimes made relationships challenging, but in time the towns were all supportive.

As the days shortened and fall arrived in earnest, the pace of activity picked up. Volunteers would come and go from the Poletti house, where the kitchen table was the nexus of the new event. Daughter Isabelle and son-in-law Mickaël created a website for which Catherine wrote the copy. The team found volunteers to translate it into four languages: Spanish, English, Italian, and German. Out in the field, Michel Poletti was busy with reconnaissance, identifying paths that could replace pavement. He searched out routes between Col de Voza and Les Contamines, and Trient and Vallorcine. Between Lac Combal and Courmayeur, Poletti found an old mountain path below Mount Favre. He dubbed the section Arête du Mont Favre, a name still used today. Searching old maps, he found faint traces of a beautiful high point above Chamonix, "Tête aux Vents," a name he brought back into use—meaning, roughly, the home of the winds. In Italy's Val Ferret, just after Courmayeur, the race was forced onto valley roads, as the Italian authorities were unnerved by what might happen if fatigued trail runners were forced to follow trails during the night.

In December 2002, the Polettis got a surprise in the mail: the very first paper application to the race, along with a check. Their goal was to find three hundred entrants. "In those days, you would register right before the race," remembers Catherine. But by spring, entries were pouring in from as far away as Australia. They began to dream of reaching five hundred entries.

A lot of questions remained, but the fledgling organization had already realized one accomplishment: there would be plenty of runners at the start line come August 30, 2003.

And they had a name: Ultra-Trail International du Tour du Mont-Blanc.

Along the way, Catherine and Michel discovered a new passion. "To create... that is the most interesting thing you can do," said Catherine. "We saw that we liked organizing something new," adds Michel. "And now we had the confidence to organize something big."

TO BE DONE!

"Just don't be stupid," Katie Schide thought to herself as she ran into Chamonix more than 1 hour and 15 minutes in front of the second-place woman, and only 3 hours and 25 minutes behind Kilian Jornet, who finished first in the men's race.

As Schide ran toward the finish line on August 27, 2022, it felt unreal to her. Spectators lined the route starting several kilometers away from the finish, as the trail widened and tilted down to town from the Balcon Sud, 800 meters above the valley. Rue Joseph Vallot was thronged with thousands of cheering fans. As she passed under the high-tech finish-line arch, hundreds of cameras and dozens of journalists recorded her every

move. Schide and other top runners were greeted by "Conquest of Paradise" echoing from towers of speakers next to the Jumbotron in Place du Triangle de l'Amitié.

The crowd at the finish roared, but all Katie Schide wanted was to sit down and not have to race any more. To be done.

Twenty-three hours, fifteen minutes, and twelve seconds after starting the UTMB, she got her wish, thanks, in part, to what she now calls her "magic cheese sandwich." A photo taken after the finish shows the thirty-year-old, introverted American woman who had relocated to France, with her hands cupped in front of her mouth, a look of disbelief across her face.

Schide finished shortly after 5 p.m. on Saturday. After the first edition, the race had shifted its start time to Friday evening, allowing slower runners more time to finish during daylight hours on Sunday. When Schide crossed the finish line, there were still over 2,200 runners out on the course. Many were only halfway done with their UTMB. By the official end of the race, 46.5 hours after its start, nearly a thousand of them would have dropped out. In the hours between Schide's finish and that of the last official finisher, Japan's Tomio Suyama, on Sunday afternoon, human dramas would play out across the trails around Mont Blanc in France, Italy, and Switzerland: injury, sickness, and deep fatigue, but also individual stories of unheralded perseverance, resilience, and fierce determination.

UTMB crowns champions and breaks hearts. Since its first edition, the race through three countries and around Mont Blanc has been filled with some of the most dramatic moments of any sport, anywhere. In the men's race, Jornet set a course record of 19:49:30, the first time anyone had gone under the 20-hour mark on the full course. Walmsley, who had moved to France from Flagstaff, Arizona with the specific goal of winning UTMB, finished fourth in 21:12:12. After, he was philosophical. "I don't necessarily worry as much about the outcome. I'm putting as much into it as a human as I can. That makes me pretty confident." He promised he would be back.

René Bachelard was there at the finish. These days, he can walk through the crowds at UTMB and only a few cognoscenti know who he is, or his importance to the race. And that's just fine with him. "I don't need people to talk about me. I took the first step, but others created it. It's incredible what UTMB is now. They took this to a global scale," he told me. "Three countries in one race. I thought it could be legendary." Bachelard saw early the differing skills that Catherine and Michel Poletti brought to the race. "Catherine had business sense. Michel had a sense for organizing events and for technology." Bachelard was one of the founders and the first president of the non-profit arm of UTMB, Les Trailers du Mont-Blanc. He is modest about his role. "I had nothing to do with it. I've always just been a volunteer."

Katie Schide's race might not have happened at all, had the hours after 4 a.m. on August 30, 2003, not gone well. Amazingly, at the close of registration for that first edition, the Polettis hadn't merely signed up the three hundred, or even the five hundred runners they had dreamed of. Seven hundred twenty-two people had registered for the first edition of the UTMB.

They had thought of almost everything. But there was one thing that was very much not in their favor and entirely out of their control: the weather. And as race day drew near, the forecast could hardly have been worse.

RENÉ BACHELARD: "CAN WE ORGANIZE A RACE LIKE THAT?"

René Bachelard has lived the last 26 years in Chamonix. A general in the French army, he retired from his military career in 1989, and from a second career as a construction manager eight years later. In 1997, he and his wife Dany moved to Chamonix. Bachelard started running at age 60. He served as president of Chamonix's trail running club, CMBM, from 1998 through 2006, and President of Les Trailers du Mont-Blanc, UTMB's nonprofit sister organization, for 13 years, from its creation in 2004 until 2016.

Before the Mont Blanc Tunnel burned in 1999, the Chamonix Club des Sports organized a race called the Tour du Mont-Blanc Ultra Marathon. It was a 7-runner relay. When the Mont Blanc Tunnel fire happened, they paused the race, since access to the other side of the mountain was too challenging.

They tried to restart that race in 2002 when the tunnel was reopened. But the sign-up numbers were low. So they just canceled it. It was a real shame!

I knew that there were people who had done the whole tour of Mont Blanc, just two friends together, in around 25 hours. So we knew it was possible to go all the way around. We wondered, could we organize a race like that?

Michel can tell you, I was a big pain in the ass because I kept asking everyone, "Can we do the Tour of Mont-Blanc? Can we do a race on the Tour of Mont-Blanc?"

I was bugging everyone. Finally in the end, Michel was like "Fine, let's have a meeting."

Catherine and Michel were available to work on this project, so the two of them were able to start the new Ultra-Trail International du Tour du Mont-Blanc. I did some of the work, but it was mostly them.

For the first edition, I was at the start line in Chamonix and I ran to Courmayeur, the shortest of the race distances. There were three stopping points for the first edition—Courmayeur, Champex-Lac, and Cha-

monix. And when I arrived in Courmayeur, I was pretty surprised. I thought that was pretty good for me!

At the end of 2003, we decided to structure things differently. We called it the Ultra-Trail du Mont-Blanc and we created the Autour Du Mont Blanc, which would organize the business end of the race, and Les Trailers du Mont Blanc, the nonprofit, to support the non-profit aspects of the race.

The Club des Sports managed all the different sports in Chamonix, but the new race was a lot for them, and they couldn't work on this race as well as we were able to. They didn't have the means to do it right. It might not seem that way from the outside now, but that's the way it was. I worked as a volunteer. We made all of the course markers and prepared all of the race bibs, and marked the race course. There was a whole lot of work behind the scenes.

Today in Chamonix, trail running has really surpassed other sports. And it brings a huge number of people to the region. People who aren't interested in running complain about all of the people who show up, who get in the way. People who are from Chamonix feel like it is detrimental to the town. That, somehow, Chamonix is no longer a mountain town. Of course, there are still tons of people who come here for skiing and climbing, but trail running is now number one. And it's because of the Tour du Mont-Blanc. People usually did the tour in 7 or 8 days. And now, they can do it in one day. It's legendary.

KARLA VALLADARES: "IT WAS LIKE FAMILY"

In 2003, as UTMB was just getting started, Karla Valladares was The North Face's Marketing Manager for Western Europe. She immediately saw potential in UTMB and was the first connection between the Polettis and The North Face. She worked with The North Face and the Polettis for years building the race and now, two decades later, still volunteers as a passionate finish line announcer.

I was in Chamonix for the Marathon du Mont-Blanc, and Catherine and Michel Poletti had a little table in the Nordic ski center with the other exhibitors. They had a map of Mont Blanc. They had little homemade brochures and were talking about the event.

I thought it was just hiking, so I asked Michel, "How many days?" He goes, "Not days, hours." I tried to picture that in my head and I said, "That's not possible."

He looked at me and said, "Of course it is."

I asked him so many questions. How many kilometers? How many people do you think you're going to have? What about checkpoints and drinks? Do you have people working for you? I was asking him all these questions and I didn't even tell them why. They thought I wanted to run.

We spoke for half an hour and then I said, "Hey, do you have a sponsor?"

Catherine said, "No, we don't have a sponsor." I told them to give me 6 hours. Just don't talk to another brand. I told them to trust me. We shook hands and just like that, I fell in love with it.

I knew this was going to be big. I saw the runners in my mind and thought, people are going to love this. This is a great opportunity, not only for The North Face, but also for runners around the world. I went to my room and I wrote down everything they had told me. Then I called Franco Fogliato and Topher Gaylord. I said, "It's going to be a great event. Please. Trust me. I know what I'm talking about."

Topher replied, "Karla, stay right there. You tell them that we are going to come and that The North Face is going to support the event." Topher and his wife Kim ran part of the Tour du Mont-Blanc from Champex to Chamonix, met up with the Polettis, and that day they shook hands with Catherine and Michel at their home around the table. It was like family.

The first edition was electrifying. We met with Dawa at Courmayeur and I remember he was just sitting down with his arms on his knees and he said to me, "I didn't think it was going to be this hard, but it's incredible."

↑ FEDERICO GILARDI AT GRAND COL FERRET, 2019 ↓ GRAND COL FERRET, 2019

FEDERICO GILARDI: "A LOT OF NICE MOMENTS"

Since 2017, Chamonix resident Federico Gilardi has been the point person at Grand Col Ferret (2537 m), the highest point along the UTMB course and one of the most brutal parts of the course. Runners, who have just finished climbing 754 meters, sometimes have to battle freezing rain, snow, high winds, and whiteout conditions.

I participated in the UTMB races for the first time in 2008, running the CCC, UTMB's 101 km race, which started in 2006. During registration for 2008, all the places for UTMB sold out in three minutes. I remember at 8 p.m., when registration opened for CCC, I felt a moment of uncertainty. It felt like "tic-tic-tic-waPOW! Yes! I'm in!"

The CCC was my third trail race ever. We had really bad weather conditions. I finished in around 25 hours and I told myself, "Never again!" Two weeks later, I started training for the next CCC, 2009.

2009 was also when I started volunteering. The first two years, I worked distributing race bibs. Then for four years I worked with one of the official photographers, driving all around the course. It was really stressful and exhausting, going from place to place in the mountains, continuously for a week. Now, they have two volunteers doing that job. In 2017, I switched to Grand Col Ferret. I've been in charge of that post ever since.

Up at the Col, we have two volunteers— me and a friend who has also volunteered since 2017—plus one or two nurses and a doctor. We have a big tent for first aid work, and we have two huge plexiglas boxes for the volunteers. We can put people in them to get them warm if they need it.

It's strange for me to see how some of these runners can arrive at our station and be so inexperienced. They've earned all the stones to get into the lottery to run UTMB or CCC, and yet I've had to teach runners how to put on their emergency blanket or explain why they should change into a dry shirt.

Even some of the top runners have shocked me. They'll arrive at Grand Col Ferret practically without having eaten anything since the start of the race. I remember in 2018, a top French runner, Caroline Chaverot, arrived in the Col completely exhausted. I asked her why she was feeling so bad and she said, "I've only eaten two peanuts since the beginning." One hundred kilometers on two peanuts!

We've had a lot of nice moments up there. One I always think about is an Asian runner who arrived at the Col completely frozen. I tried to offer him something. "Hot tea?" "No, no, no." "Some Coke?" "No." "Water?" "No." "Red wine?" "Oh, YES, red wine, please!"

I filled his cup with red wine, he drank it, and said, "I'm well now, thank you! Bye!" And he continued on his way down into Switzerland.

Another really nice moment was in 2021. There was a group who made the trip around Mont Blanc, before the race. They had an all-terrain, one-wheeled stretcher and were transporting a runner who was gravely ill. They spent 20 minutes with us and we gave them pasta with wild garlic pesto, *l'ail des ours*. Their friend, the runner who was being carried, was so happy. He was crying.

Over a number of days, the group traveled all the way around Mont Blanc. They told us later that our little party was a highlight of their tour. The runner passed away a few months later. It was one of the most touching moments I've had volunteering up at the Col.

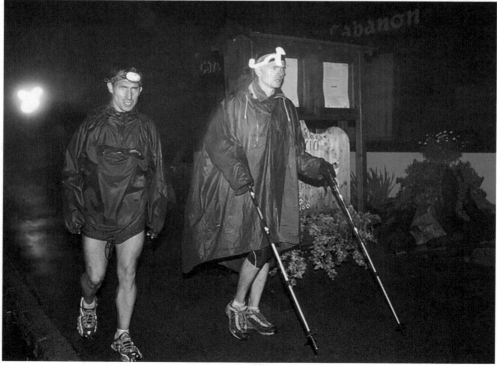

PLACE BALMAT, CHAMONIX, FRANCE. AUGUST 30, 2003, 4:00 A.M.

Throughout August 2003, newspapers around the world were talking about the intense heatwave that had gripped all of Europe. It was, incredibly, the hottest summer since 1540, and France was hit particularly hard, with more than fourteen thousand fatalities attributed to the heat. In some areas of the country, temperatures remained at 100 degrees Fahrenheit for more than a week.

Back home in Seattle, Washington, a young American trail runner named Krissy Moehl was packing for a new European trail race. Reading the news, Moehl wasn't particularly worried about the weather. She packed lightly.

Twenty-five years old, Moehl had just discovered trail running and was part of a new pro team called Montrail, a bilingual portmanteau of "Mont" and "Trail": "Mountain Trail." The trip was a honeymoon, in fact—a wedding gift to Moehl and her husband from Montrail company CEO Menno Van Wyk, who was excited by the idea of this new race around Mont Blanc. Moehl would take part, as would her husband Brandon Sybrowsky, who was also on the Montrail Team.

Moehl and Sybrowsky arrived in Chamonix on Thursday evening, just two days before the race. On Friday morning, she looked out of her bedroom window. Craning her neck, she saw the snow-covered summits. "I thought, 'Oh, wow.' The severity of the vertical profile was a big reality check."

There was a hitch, too: the longest race Moehl had ever run was 100 kilometers. This race was another 50 km longer, with much more climbing, and on more technical terrain. It would test her limits.

Later that Friday, the weather flipped as a cold front raced across Europe. The temperature plummeted, clouds moved in, and it began to rain.

Moehl went to a shop in town and purchased gloves, a beanie, and a lightweight rain shell. Weather forecasts were ominous. "They were predicting a crazy storm the night of the race," she said.

That Friday, Safety Director Pierre Faussurier called a meeting of his team. The forecast was not improving: driving rain, snow, and high winds were in the offing. They made the decision to eliminate a 2,665-meter-high pass called Col des Fours, which would have been the highest point on the course. Instead, runners would descend to the French hamlet of Les Chapieux. It was a course change that would stick for all ensuing editions.

What would happen out on the course? Poletti and others knew it was humanly possible to run around Mont Blanc in one go—but for how many of the more than seven hundred starters? For the race organizers, it was an open question. Taking a cue from a race Michel Poletti had participated in the year before, the group proposed three official finish lines: Courmayeur, Champex-Lac, and Chamonix. Moehl, for her part, wanted to go the distance. "I'm pretty stubborn," she explained.

The weather in Chamonix at 4:00 a.m. on August 30, 2003, was miserable. Skies were overcast and rainy, and the wind howled through town. On the higher elevations of the course, 1,000 meters above town, snow was falling.

PRE-EXISTING RACES

SELECT ULTRA TRAIL RACES AROUND THE WORLD THAT PRE-DATED UTMB MONT BLANC

1 — **1974**

WESTERN STATES ENDURANCE RUN, CALIFORNIA, USA

161 km/100.2 miles   5,486 meters/18,000 feet

2 — **1983**

LEADVILLE TRAIL 100, COLORADO, USA

161 km/100 miles   4,799 meters/15,744 feet

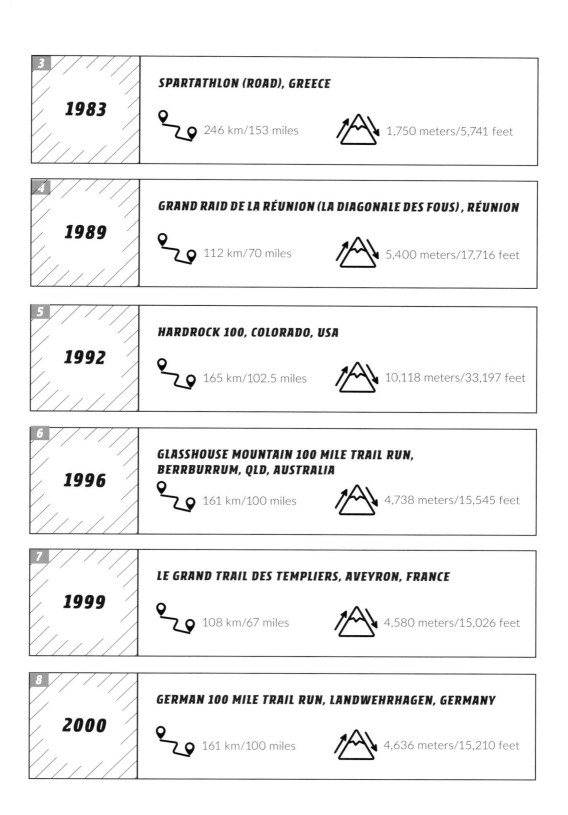

3

1983

SPARTATHLON (ROAD), GREECE

246 km/153 miles   1,750 meters/5,741 feet

4

1989

GRAND RAID DE LA RÉUNION (LA DIAGONALE DES FOUS), RÉUNION

112 km/70 miles   5,400 meters/17,716 feet

5

1992

HARDROCK 100, COLORADO, USA

165 km/102.5 miles   10,118 meters/33,197 feet

6

1996

GLASSHOUSE MOUNTAIN 100 MILE TRAIL RUN, BERRBURRUM, QLD, AUSTRALIA

161 km/100 miles   4,738 meters/15,545 feet

7

1999

LE GRAND TRAIL DES TEMPLIERS, AVEYRON, FRANCE

108 km/67 miles   4,580 meters/15,026 feet

8

2000

GERMAN 100 MILE TRAIL RUN, LANDWEHRHAGEN, GERMANY

161 km/100 miles   4,636 meters/15,210 feet

Among those at the starting line that day were other notable participants, including a thirty-three-year-old Nepali who had relocated to Switzerland eight years earlier, Dawa Sherpa. Sherpa, a high-mountain guide who had spent seven years in a Buddhist monastery, had run a few trail races in the Alps, and was a friend of both Catherine and Michel Poletti. Sherpa already knew parts of the course, having run from Champex-Lac to Trient as part of the Tour du Mont-Blanc Ultra Marathon relay back in 1996. Also at the starting line: Christopher "Topher" Gaylord, an American who was representing a new marquee sponsor, The North Face (see Karla Vallardes' memory on page 48).

Several of the volunteer organizers were at the starting line on the day of the race, most notably "The Three Musketeers," as Catherine called them: Michel Poletti, René Bachelard, and Jean-Claude Marmier, the retired head of France's mountain troops. Bachelard planned to stop in Courmayeur, but Poletti wanted to go the distance. And Marmier? "Jean-Claude," remembered Catherine Poletti, "was not going to stop."

THE TRAIL

You would think the start would be the easiest part of running 100 miles around Mont Blanc, but it's arguably the most dangerous. Wildly cheering spectators line the street, and the barricades barely keep them from spilling into the fast-flowing stream of runners.

Then there are the trail-running poles. Katie Schide calls it a "polenado," a tornado of pointy carbon-fiber poles. At UTMB, nearly all runners bring them, and many start with them in hand. So close to others, it's easy to get stabbed, poked, or simply tripped up by the dreaded polenado.

From time to time, a few runners fall here, and one or two have ended their UTMB before it has even really started.

For the first kilometer, there is always a little-known runner out front. He—and it is always a he—seeks the attention of the crowds and the chance to be immortalized in the iconic start photos, perhaps relishing the idea of leading thousands of runners out into the mountains.

Somewhere outside of town, perhaps after the Gaillands cliff where novice climbers practice their moves on a top-rope, the vibe shifts. There's room to breathe, the fans are few and far between, and the runners begin to settle into a pace that they hope to hell will work for the next twenty... thirty... forty or more hours.

For kilometers 2 through 10, UTMB is practically playful, like the easiest beginner's trail race course one could find. A wide gravel track rolls gently alongside the Arve River as it meanders down the valley to the village of Les Houches. Here, the valley says "au revoir" to the runners, as they head up the first ascent, 690 meters to the grassy pastures at Col de Voza. It will be on average about 38 hours before the runners reach the Chamonix valley again. Although all runners need to have finished at least one 100-kilometer trail race to register, at least 30% of them will drop out before the finish line. UTMB is a different beast.

After the climb, it's a speedy, easy run down a wide track to the village of St. Gervais, famous for its support of the race. While dwarfed by the numbers in Chamonix, the spectators at this mountain town at the meeting point of the Chamonix and Les Contamines valleys make up for their smaller numbers with their boisterousness. It's UTMB's first aid station, and already the pack is spread out, with slower runners coming in as the blanket of darkness begins to settle over the mountains. Once through the aid station, a rolling dozen kilometers brings runners to a critical moment in their UTMB experience: Notre Dame de la Gorge.

Here, where a chapel has stood for a thousand years, UTMB gets down to business. If the race has been almost carefree for the 35 kilometers since Chamonix, it now gets deadly serious. A 1,200-meter climb awaits, culminating in one of the course's more challenging high traverses at Col de la Croix du Bonhomme. This is why runners come, for the challenge, and to see what will remain as their veneer starts to get ripped away. If their mind is in the right place, their answer to the course is, "Okay, UTMB, bring it on." If it's not, they're getting scared.

But there is one last moment of conviviality. Each year, the locals build a bonfire at Notre Dame de la Gorge. Génépi, the Alpine herbal liqueur made from the plant of the same name, is passed around. There's singing, cheering, and smiles as the steep climb up the old Roman road begins. In 2022 HOKA installed a LED tube (see photo page 61) that raised some eyebrows.

The once-packed horde of runners is now an elongating serpent, wending its way out of the forest, along farm roads, and finally onto a technical single-track above tree line. Thousands of headlamps weave and bob, illuminating the course for kilometers. The spectacle is dramatic, the kind of scene that causes most runners to stop at some moment during the climb to take it all in. On the ground, conversations have ended, oxygen fully dedicated to the work at hand. There is grunting, sniffling, sighing... the sounds of muscle-powered work.

On average, in the mountains, the temperature drops 6.5 degrees Celsius for every 1,000 meters, or about 5.4 degrees Fahrenheit per thousand feet. Scientists call this the adiabatic lapse rate, and it is one of the drivers of mountain weather, leading to clouds as air rises and cools. For UTMB runners reaching the rocky traverse at Col du Bonhomme, it often means it's time to stop and don a wind shell, hat, and gloves.

By this time, it is completely dark, and the sun won't rise again until 6:30 a.m. In fact, elite runners will run almost half of their race in the dark. Many of the less elite will see the night twice. Though lamps shine brightly along the course, running at night is a solitary activity. There is just the sound of one's breathing, and vision is limited to a dancing cone of light on the trail ahead. Enough attention is required that the mind ceases to wander, and as the hours pass, running becomes a meditation of sorts. Occasionally, objects passed on the periphery surprise: a signpost, a bench, a shepherd's hut, perhaps even a racer sorting gear or quietly taking a time out.

In poor weather, getting across the traverse between Col du Bonhomme and the Col de la Croix du Bonhomme can be dicey. The sidehill

traverse is rocky and uneven, and the terrain affords no shelter from the vagaries of the mountain weather. Forward progress can be slow. In time, though, the trail eases onto pasture, ending with a cruisy descent to the aid station at Les Chapieux—even if the notoriously sharp rocks that jut up require undivided attention. Here, the US runner Tim Tollefson fell in 2018. One of the world's best and well beyond tough, Tollefson managed to run for another 90 kilometers with blood slowly draining from a wound that would later require ten stitches.

It's hard to imagine that the remote mountain outpost of Les Chapieux, home to a few dozen houses and two mountain inns, was once on the front line of World War II battles. Here, in a fierce battle on August 15, 1944, French resistance fighters ambushed a German convoy. UTMB runners pass, most of them unaware of the stone-built machine-gun emplacements in the side of the hill and the plaque just a few meters away commemorating Le Combat des Chapieux.

UTMB rolls onward up a lush valley alongside the Torrent des Glaciers, where it's not unusual for one's headlamp to flash upon sleepy cows lying in adjacent pastures. A steady, smooth climb to the French–Italian border at Col de la Seigne comes next. Were it daytime here, runners might see all the way to Grand Col Ferret, still hours away on their journey.

In fair weather, UTMB diverts from a downhill cruise to take in Pyramides Calcaires, a challenging extra 1.6 kilometers that puts the UTMB course climbing over five figures. These bonus meters are the first to be dropped if the weather threatens, however.

From here, the course relents. There's a downhill cruise past Rifugio Elisabetta, a popular stop for Tour du Mont-Blanc hikers with a reputation for hearty polenta and fresh blueberry tarts. Perhaps the only truly flat section in the entire course is next, a Roman road alongside Lac Combal. It's a chance to run carefree, though for most UTMB runners, this section becomes a personal war against circadian programming. Eyelids become heavy, brains foggy. But because of their experience qualifying in earlier long-distance races, runners know it will not last. In a few hours, the first rays of light will hit their retinas, their brains will acknowledge the reality of a new day, and they will find renewed energy.

After a brief climb—and only in a race like UTMB can 457 meters be considered brief—UTMB relents again, presenting runners with a rolling downhill cruise to Maison Vieille. At this well-known aid station, Giacomo Calosi and his staff pass the night dishing out bowls of pasta to runners who are now starting to split into the only two groups that matter: those who will finish and those who will not.

The highest gravity location—by which I mean, the location that tempts runners to stop and makes it hardest for them to get going again—comes next, after a dusty and steep descent to the race's almost-midpoint in Courmayeur. "Get in and get out," top US runner David Laney once told me, and it's good advice. With its cots and offers of free massages, the enormous aid station at the Dolonne sports center, just across the Dora Baltea River from town, has a way of luring the undertrained into pulling the bibs off their shirts and falling into a deep sleep.

Most continue, however—up the steep 816-meter climb to Rifugio Bertone, along the smooth, rolling balcony past Rifugio Bonatti, and down to the valley aid station at Arnouva. "Don't look up," a fellow runner once told me here, and he was right. Grand Col Ferret looms above, and even if your race is going as planned, it's hard not to feel gut-punched as your head cranes upward in search of the climb's end.

In time, though, runners finish the smooth switchbacks to the Col, perhaps noticing the slightly thinner air. Federico Gilardi (see page 51) or one of his team cheer them on, down the fastest part of the UTMB course, running past herds of cows and sheep. Runners often go faster than they should here, and the results of cutting loose become painfully apparent in their quads at the next aid station, in the Swiss village of La Fouly.

Here, as is true at aid stations all along the course, cameras and timing mats record runners' passage for friends and family around the world. Soon, as they run downward alongside the Dranse de Ferret River, the cliffs of the Mont Blanc massif on their left, they may receive texts from far-flung supporters.

Rare stretches of pavement come next, tenderizing quads that have already endured 112 kilometers through the Alps. At this point the runners are more than halfway done in terms of distance and vertical, if not of time. But it's still far too early to get confident about seeing Chamonix again, for there are four big climbs yet to come.

The first leads up to Champex-Lac. Many UTMB dreams end here, in the huge tent where pastry chef and bakery owner Léon Lovey is still the "Chef de Poste." As runners leave, UTMB officials might stop them for a gear check, asking to see a rain shell, or the two required headlamps, since for many participants the next section brings a second sleepless night. That second *nuit blanche* is likely to be much harder than the first, as a frontal cortex miswired from lack of sleep and fuel generates fantastical thoughts and quirky hallucinations. At this point in the race, during my first UTMB, I thought I was on a rescue mission with friends in New Hampshire's White Mountains. Ten years and 5,900 kilometers mentally off base, the fantasy helped pass the hours.

Next comes a widely vilified section of the course—a rocky, endless-feeling, charmless climb on rock-strewn farm tracks. Here, it's hard not to think of Winston Churchill's advice: "If you're going through hell, keep going." In two hours, runners reach the pasture gate above Bovine, signaling the start of the long descent to Trient, a Swiss village of just 145 inhabitants nestled down, down, down in the deepest of troughs in the wrinkled fabric that is the Alps. Fortunately, Trient during UTMB is a rowdy party scene, and lucky runners may hear the band playing long before they arrive at the famous pink church just a few meters from the aid station.

Runners must dig deep and find some energy here, because getting out of Trient involves 785 meters of climbing—all of it steep. After another hour, in the high pastures of Catogne, they might begin to dream of friends, family, and maybe even a bottle of champagne in Chamonix. But they know better. There are still 23 kilometers to go, including one of the hardest climbs of the race.

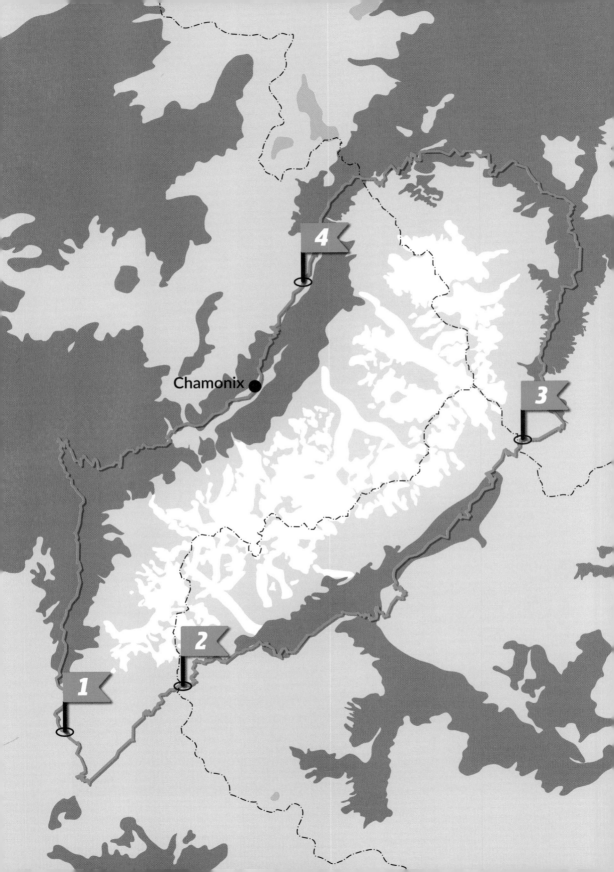

THE HARDEST CLIMBS

1. COL DE LA CROIX DU BONHOMME
Ascent: 1,329 m/4,327 ft, High point: 2,479 m/8,133 ft

The second significant mountain climb in the UTMB journey, this is a big one. In fact, it has the most amount of vertical in one continuous climb of any of the climbs along the UTMB course. There are hints of what's to come, starting as early as St. Gervais, where the course begins to tilt ever so slightly upwards. Then, at about 35 km into the race, the climb begins in earnest. Most runners reach the start of this upward push at the beginning of the first night. Spectators have a huge bonfire, music, and they line the start of the climb, cheering for the runners—all of which makes for an exciting and energetic send-off into one of the more wild sections of the race course. Tackling this climb in the dark with rocky terrain can be as much of a mental effort as a physical one.

2. COL DE LA SEIGNE AND COL DES PYRAMIDES CALCAIRES
Ascent: 958 m/3,143 ft, High point: 2,567 m/8,422 ft

Col de la Seigne plus nearby Col des Pyramides Calcaires takes you to the highest altitude on the course. If the weather is bad, this crossing into Italy can be one of the most severe on the course because of its full-on exposure to the weather.

3. GRAND COL FERRET
Ascent: 754 m/2,474 ft, High point: 2,537 m/8,323 ft

This is the second highest point on the UTMB course. While the climb itself isn't as much ascent as others, it's steep, climbing 754 meters in just 4.5 km. Getting to the Col often results in a full-on but brief exposure to wind, fog and sometimes even snow.

4. TÊTE AUX VENTS
Ascent: 863 m/2,831 ft, High point: 2,130 m/6,988 ft

The final climb of the UTMB course feels worse because of the 153 km and 9070 m runners have already tackled. Less than 20 km from the finish, this climb takes runners to one of the most beautiful spots on the course. And after? There's not much standing in the way of getting to Chamonix.

Somewhere around here, in a spot unknown to runners, they cross without fanfare back onto French soil, running down through magnificent pastures that they can only barely grasp are, in fact, quite beautiful. The aid station of Vallorcine awaits, and it's not advisable to drop here unless you literally cannot make forward progress. Those who DNF ("did not finish") under the tent in Vallorcine are truly in crisis, perhaps unable to keep food down, or injured and incapable of even a gentle jog. Everyone else—walking wounded included—knows they are closing in on one of the greatest accomplishments of their lifetime. Of course, there are many reasons that runners stop. Injuries are the most common, including blisters so severe they make walking nearly impossible. Others suffer from rounds of vomiting that drain every calorie available just when it is most needed. Rarer are more serious conditions, like the massive drop in salt levels known as hyponatremia that can lead to unconsciousness, or bouts of quasi-hallucinations triggered by two nights without sleep.

Next comes a deceivingly uphill 3.7 kilometers. It might seem flat, but the steady grade is cruel enough that a few of UTMB's top runners have dubbed it the "asshole hill." It's mean-spirited, allowing for no rest before Col des Montets, a quick road crossing, and what just might be the hardest climb of a runner's life.

On any other day, the passage into the Réserve Naturelle des Aiguilles Rouges would cause anyone to stop and stare. Even though Route D1506 between Argentière and Vallorcine passes through this high valley, it's a wild spot. In winter, avalanches sweep off the steep walls, closing off the high pass. Ibex and chamois watch over the terrain, cached amid the cliffs and boulders. At this point, though, runners may be further into the pain cave than they have ever found themselves, in a remote and dark corner where it's too fatiguing even to say hello to the enthusiastic hikers cheering them on. These hikers might smell of fresh deodorant, while the runners passing them stink of sweat and dirt. But the runners run on, doing what they first learned to do: put one foot in front of the other and not fall.

Here, elite runners push themselves as hard as humanly possible. David Laney of Bellingham, Washington (see page 175), who has had multiple podium finishes at UTMB, describes his experience like this: "It's a feedback loop. It's a sort of nuclear fusion. I take the discomfort, and I channel it into pure energy. Energy becomes more energy, and it all goes towards running harder. It's not like it doesn't hurt, though. It's extremely painful."

It was in this location, during the 2015 edition of UTMB, that that fusion almost spiraled out of control. The Alps on that race day were scorching hot. Laney, who a few months later would be crowned *UltraRunning Magazine's* Ultra Runner of the Year, worried that he was developing heat stroke. "I thought to myself, this is how you die," he remembered later. Where the trail crossed a small creek, Laney lay down in the water, face first. "People were staring at me, wondering if I was okay." Laney recovered and went on to finish third. At the mandatory drug testing for top finishers, he passed out.

Eventually, though, the climbing tapers out at Tête aux Vents, with—other than a token climb to Flégère—the work finally done. Below, the Chamonix valley is at your feet. Runners might allow themselves to dare imagine the finish line. The sounds, the crowds, the applause, one's name being called out. If they have any energy to spare, they can look up at Mont Blanc, now in its full glory. (If it's daytime, and there are no clouds.) After a stop at the final aid station, all that remains is a woodsy 8-kilometer cruise into town.

For many runners, this is a time to reflect. After dozens of hours, they may find themselves deeply introspective, even if the thoughts are not coherent or well-formed. Soon, they begin to comprehend, it will be time to return to the mundane world below. To try explain this experience to their families, however hard it may be. After all, they've just come back from a world most people cannot even imagine.

It would be convenient to say that all runners returning to Chamonix at the end of UTMB share the same experience. But the reality is, the experiences are different and sometimes markedly so. Some arrive in the middle of the night, greeted by small but enthusiastic throngs of friends. Many find new energy, perhaps the result of what physiologists call the "Central Governor Theory." This theory states that the brain controls the sense of fatigue and manages the body to avoid a catastrophic outcome. But as runners make the final turn onto Rue Vallot, they are done, for all intents and purposes, and their brains know it. They turn the exhaustion off. Runners can now run fast without courting disaster. And many do.

And then, incomprehensibly, suddenly, somehow, they have done it. It is happening. They hear their name announced. They see friends, spot a look of wonderment in their eyes. Perhaps they look down, not quite ready to meet the stares of others. Tears might be forming. Their UTMB is over.

That, in a few pages, is what it is like to run UTMB.

But nearly everything was different back in 2003, except for the most important thing. Save for a few revisions here and there, the trail was still very much the same, as was the physical and mental challenge it presented.

Perhaps the biggest difference between the first edition and all that followed was the simple reality that the outcome on that morning in August 2003 was anything but certain.

A SIMPLE COUNTDOWN

"It was," Michel Poletti tells me, recalling the first edition, "a dream come true." It was also Poletti's father's eightieth birthday, and his son David's sixteenth. At the briefing the day before the race at Chamonix's Centre Sportif, the group wished the elderly Poletti a happy eightieth. "It was quite emotional," Poletti said.

As the racers gathered, so did the spectators. Krissy Moehl began to realize how different the vibe was in Europe. "In the US, it was all very homegrown. Everyone racing would have just one degree of separation.

Races were organized out of someone's garage. Here were over seven hundred racers and—even for this first edition—spectators lining the street at 4 a.m. In Europe, even then, trail racing was a spectator sport."

Race director Catherine Poletti gave a simple countdown through a microphone. There was no music and not much fanfare when, a few moments after 4:00 a.m., 722 runners set off into the darkness, wind, and rain, headlamps glowing, turning left onto Rue du Dr. Paccard and heading out of town. Volunteers who had been at the start line raced to their cars to get to the checkpoints along the first 30 kilometers of the race course.

Catherine Poletti was left behind with two radios, a Nokia flip phone, a laptop, and several volunteers. "We felt very alone at the start line," she remembers. "There were just a few of us."

For the next forty hours, she remained on the bridge, sheltered under the bus stop booth and a 10x10-foot tent that served as the race's main control point. Using a homemade database designed by Michel, Catherine entered names and locations of runners as they were radioed in from around Mont Blanc.

For Moehl, despite the stormy conditions, the race started well. She connected with a German runner, Ludwig. The two spoke in Spanish, their one shared language, during the long hours on the course. The beginning was fast. "It was cruisy," she said. But at Notre Dame, Moehl hit her first real challenge. "It was steep and bouldery and really hard." The storm wasn't letting up. Moehl recalls cinching the hood of her new Patagonia shell tight around her face.

Despite the fierce weather, Moehl clearly remembers the spectators who braved the storm. "I was moved by the number of people outside, cheering us up the long climb in the early morning hours, in that downpour!"

One element of the race involved something she hadn't experienced in US trail races. "Runners were cutting the switchbacks, running straight down the descents. I remember wondering, 'Is that okay?'"

Along the way, Moehl encountered another surprise to her US trail running sensibilities. "I had been used to M&Ms, potato chips, peanut butter and jelly sandwiches, and Coke... and here, volunteers were handing out dried fruit, dark chocolate, huge hunks of cheese, and pieces of a baguette. There was even a wheel of raclette!"

Dawa Sherpa's race had, by and large, started off well, too. From Col du Bonhomme, he stayed in the lead, but like everyone else was battling steady rain, sleet, hail, and high winds. "I remember at the aid stations, the volunteers were taking shelter behind boulders, trying to stay out of the weather," he said. The simple aid stations offered water and sometimes broth.

Poletti also remembers crossing the 2,479-meter Col de la Croix du Bonhomme. The volunteer there was hiding behind a cairn, trying desperately to stay warm while welcoming runners and recording bib numbers. "The weather, it was insane," said Sherpa. The tempest continued for another 15 kilometers to the Italian border at Col de la Seigne. "Finally, once we were in Italy, the weather started to improve."

Ahead of Poletti, on the other side of Mont Blanc, Dawa Sherpa later ate a bowl of pasta in Courmayeur. Further along, in Champex-Lac, Sherpa was told that the second runner was an hour behind him. He stopped in the old military bunker the organization had requisitioned for the race, eating two bowls of pasta as he got a massage. Thirty minutes later, he quietly left Champex-Lac. Sherpa ran into the night, the weather moderating slightly until rain started again at Les Tseppes, high above Vallorcine. Sherpa liked the weather. "If I have a choice between sun and cold, I prefer the cold," he said. "I can keep my energy up."

At around 10 p.m. on Friday night, eighteen hours into the race, Catherine's radio came alive with reports that Dawa Sherpa was pulling into the aid station in Vallorcine. She announced the news. Unsure how long the run would take down the Chamonix valley from Vallorcine, she was perhaps a bit optimistic. "Dawa Sherpa… he's arriving!"

Word spread and spectators started to gather in the pouring rain at the finish line in Chamonix. Catherine wanted to keep them from leaving. With the help of a volunteer announcer, she talked up the crowd for two hours, doing her best to keep onlookers from wandering off into the rain.

By midnight, about a hundred people were there, with umbrellas to fend off the ceaseless rain. "I had never seen so many people there… Mayor Charlet, other elected officials… Everyone started to show up. I thought it was incredible," Catherine Poletti said.

Finally, a few minutes after midnight, Sherpa came into view. Young school kids, out with their parents, ran the final meters alongside him. "Though we didn't know each other, Karla [Valladares] (see page 48) hugged me," remembers Sherpa. "We chatted a bit. But mostly, it was pouring rain."

And so, a little past midnight on August 31, 2003, Dachhiri Dawa Sherpa became the first person to cross the line at the first edition of the Ultra-Trail International du Tour du Mont-Blanc. He had run 150 kilometers with 8,100 meters of climbing in a time of 20:05:59.

Fifteen minutes later, the crowd dispersed into the rainy night, and the finish line was deserted.

Right around this time, Krissy Moehl was pulling into the aid station in Trient, Switzerland. Ludwig stopped to smoke a cigarette and wait for sunrise. He gave his rain pants to Moehl, encouraging her to keep going.

From 12:15 a.m. onward, once again, Catherine was alone at the finish line. Partiers emptied out of the local Chamonix bars. For two hours, she waited for the next finisher. Then Topher Gaylord and Brandon Sybrowsky ran in together, tying for second. Poletti gave them tea and draped blankets over them. To this day, their shared finish remains the best of any American male trail runner at UTMB.

Moments later, Catherine's flip phone rang. It was the volunteers in Trient, Switzerland, 26 kilometers from the finish. "There's a girl here who's injured but she wants to keep going. She's worried about heading off alone, so she's going with Michel. She's the first woman. She's from the US, and her name is Krissy Moehl."

Moehl was suffering from a cascading series of injuries. She had an inflamed iliotibial band, the result of near-constant hammering on long downhills. That, in turn, triggered her foot flexor to fail on her other leg, causing her to trip frequently.

Michel Poletti was not a lot better off. At the race's high point, Grand Col Ferret, he had felt defeated, and only got up after another runner started yelling at him to get moving. In Champex-Lac, a few hours later, he had been sick, unable to eat and close to vomiting. The doctor there had tried to stop him from continuing. He was very pale. "I remember climbing up to Bovine in pouring rain. I felt like I was climbing up a river." From Bovine onward, Poletti was only able to drink Coke. "It was the first time I had Coke in an ultra," he told me with a laugh. "It was pretty good!"

Krissy Moehl was 124 kilometers into the 150-kilometer-long race. Soaking wet, she juggled maintaining her modesty with taking off her clothes, wringing the water out, and draping them over a nearby heater. She took a few minutes to eat as much as possible.

Ludwig, meanwhile, was done. He decided to stay in the church until sunrise, and later dropped out of the race. Moehl wanted to keep going but didn't want to run through the night alone. Spotting another runner, she asked if they could head out together. It was Poletti. And so, Michel Poletti and Krissy Moehl headed out into the night together, neither knowing the other, much less their respective positions in the new world of ultra-distance trail running.

Those next miles were surreal for Moehl. "I remember the cowbells during the night... my brain was not quite hallucinating but getting close. The tones were changing, they were close and far away... It all felt magical."

Meanwhile, at the finish line, Catherine explained the call she had just received to the two Americans waiting with her. "That's my new wife," explained Sybrowsky. "We're here on our honeymoon!" It was an odd and amusing flipping of partners, and to this day, Catherine jokes about it. "Michel spent the night with another woman!" she told me with a laugh. "But of course, I was there with her husband!"

And still, there was the weather. From Les Tseppes to Catogne, Poletti and Moehl battled snow and wind. "The wind was coming from the west, right into our faces. It was really difficult," Michel Poletti remembered. On the descent, Moehl's IT band would not let her run downhill. "Go on, go on," Moehl insisted. Poletti stayed with her until they reached a ski-area road, from which he knew she could safely get to the next aid station.

That first edition of the race stayed low after crossing the Swiss-French border into Vallorcine, winding its way through the valley to Chamonix. A few kilometers from the outskirts of town, in the village of Les Tines, the reality of his accomplishment started to wash over Poletti. "From Les Tines to Chamonix, I was in tears. It was incredible to be finishing. All of my emotions were pouring out." During those last minutes, however, Poletti was already thinking about the next edition. Everyone agreed the name of the race was too long and convoluted. On that run into town, he had a simple four-letter acronym in mind: U.T.M.B. The Ultra-Trail du Mont-Blanc.

At 8:31 a.m., Poletti crossed the line into the arms of his wife.

"Like everyone, in my life I had big goals," he told me. "I wanted to climb an 8,000-meter peak. I was supposed to go to climb Mount McKinley [Denali] in Alaska one year but missed it. This goal... to start in Chamonix and come back to Chamonix, the city where I was born... my land... my country... this was a ten-year dream that came true."

One hour and seven minutes after Poletti, Moehl came into town, hobbling badly. And it was cold. Moehl was wearing clothes borrowed from volunteers at aid stations. "Honestly, I was wrecked," she told me nearly twenty years later. "I was a gimpy mess."

The details of her finish at 9:38 a.m. are not etched in her mind. "I was deep inside my head," she explained. The race had taken its toll. "I was defeated physically." But not so much that she couldn't cross the finish line in a time of 29:38:23, making her the women's winner of the first edition of what would soon called the UTMB. The next female finisher, Anne-Marie Bais-Le-Roux, was more than two hours behind.

"The race that day," said Moehl, "it just beat everyone up!"

Only sixty-seven finishers crossed the line on August 31 in Chamonix. Over seven hundred others either dropped out or settled for a result in Courmayeur or Champex-Lac.

As for the starters that first year? Moehl came back four more times, dropping out twice and winning UTMB once more. In the years that followed, she went on to set course records around the world, including at Colorado's Hardrock Hundred Mile Endurance Run, and at the 170-mile-long Tahoe Rim Trail. She has raced more than one hundred ultramarathons.

Dawa Sherpa came in second the following year, fifth in 2007, second again in 2008, and in 2012 he won UTMB's TDS race. He went on to compete for Nepal in Nordic skiing in three winter Olympics, and has run over one hundred trail races.

Topher Gaylord competed in nine more UTMB races, finishing in the Top 10 three times. He raced Western States seven times and the New York Marathon five times, including one race in which he came in third in his over 50 age group. He has run over 75 ultras.

René Bachelard continued to race from time to time, running all the way up to 98 kilometers in the 2009 edition of UTMB's CCC race. In 2016, at age eighty-four, he finished UTMB's 56-kilometer OCC race. He raced the 40-km MCC race the following year and broke his shoulder. At age ninety-one, he continues to run. Friends follow him on Strava or on Facebook, where he shares his runs. "I'm not training anymore, but I force myself to get out and move every day," he told me. "I go at about 6 or 7 kilometers per hour. For you, that's a stroll. For me, it's my maximum effort. Motivation is hard. I get tired after about two hours. Fatigue arrives quickly these days."

Michel Poletti has since run another eighty or so ultras. He has started UTMB another seven times and finished six of them. Three times during various UTMB weeks, he's run the organization's TDS course. Overall, Poletti has run nearly forty races in UTMB's international series, the Ultra-Trail World Tour, and now, the new UTMB World Series races. No person has run more UTMB-associated races. Among UTMB staff, it's a point of amusement and pride: In the global race to accrue "Running Stones"—UTMB's term for lottery entries to land a coveted starting line spot in one of the August Chamonix races—no one has more stones than their boss.

TIM TOLLEFSON: "YOU'RE STILL THE SAME COMING OUT"

Success, failure, and intense pressure. Tim Tollefson has experienced it all at UTMB with his two consecutive 3rd place finishes (2016, 2017) and a series of DNFs (Did Not Finish) in 2018, 2019, 2021, and 2022. While he may not have not won the race, Tim has nonetheless gained something lasting—the wisdom to discern what matters.

I love the saying, "The sweet is never as sweet without the sour." UTMB encapsulates that idea perfectly. Every time one sets out on the course, there is a high chance of failure. And anyone who has seen success at UTMB has also likely had moments of failure or hardship out there. With UTMB, there's simply no going through the motions. But I think if something leaves you a little heartbroken at times, it probably means you're chasing the right dragon. It's a big unknown and that's a very powerful motivator. When one is fortunate enough to close the loop, the satisfaction is so rewarding.

UTMB has always been the global stage where I wanted to prove that I belong in this sport. The lure of the event is completely intoxicating. With the dramatic peaks towering over the valley and crazed, passionate fans down in each village—the experience is so dramatic and amplified. It's like being sent off on a hero's journey. And when you do finish, it's like being a gladiator who returns home, celebrated almost unjustifiably with thousands of people pouring their excitement into you. One can't help but reflect it back to the crowd. You've accomplished something that seemed insurmountable, both on paper and in your head for probably 90% of the time you were out there. It's euphoric.

But the loop is often left incomplete. In 2022, I just didn't have energy in the tank. I was redlining and the idea of unraveling for another 20 hours was overwhelming. Yet pulling out of UTMB is as emotionally and physically painful as continuing on. Hoping no one would see me, I waited until there was a break in the headlamps, turned off my own lamp, and stepped off the trail into the dark. I stood in that field, looking at the stars, trying to make my decision. It was a moment marked with a lot of shame and sadness as I accepted that my race was over.

Walking back, in the opposite direction of the runners still heading out on their hero's journey, I felt myself hiding in the shadows and covering up my logos. I didn't want people to waste their energy on me. In that moment it felt like closing the door on hope, like the world had crumbled.

In reality, it was just a single moment, a single race, a single day of my life. It's so important to separate this event, and this sport, from one's worth as a person. I have definitely fallen victim to this trap—having my identity so tied up in the outcome that a failure at UTMB felt like a failure as a person. I used to believe that if I won UTMB, I would have finally "made it" or been able to change myself, but now I see that even if I had won, I would have still felt empty.

The reality is that you're not going to change as a result of any of these adventures. Whoever you are going in, you're still the same coming out, but you can learn more about yourself and hopefully grow from it. You can learn to smile at your monsters.

Everything in life is impermanent, imperfect and incomplete. And that's how I feel about my life with UTMB. I try to embrace it all—redefining success and reframing failure. There is no perfect day, everyone struggles and has to overcome something. Sometimes the journey feels especially imperfect or incomplete, but I keep showing up and giving the best of myself. I think that that's all any of us can do. That's the win.

DAWA SHERPA: "WHY NOT, I'LL TRY!"

In the year that started it all, 2003, Dawa Sherpa holds the honor of being the inaugural UTMB men's winner during his first continuous 100-mile run. He went on to run UTMB five times: 2003 (1st), 2004 (2nd), 2007 (5th), 2008 (2nd), 2010 (11th). The Nepal-born mountain trail runner shares moments from his journey—from first learning to trail run in Nepal to his more recent passion for gardening at home in France.

I was used to hiking as a mountain guide, carrying a heavy load or backpack, but I didn't have any experience with running. It was quite surprising how difficult it was for me to run in the mountains at first. My muscles hurt so much! But after two or three days I got used to it.

I didn't have any time to train before my first race or even know what gear to carry. Just a few days before the race, I went to the market in Kathmandu and bought some shoes that the shopkeeper said were good for running. I paid 1500 rupees, which was nearly one month's salary. After about three days, the shoes were already falling apart.

But I got so much from that first race. I found two great loves. First, I found my love of trail running. It's such a simple sport. When we are in nature, there are no strict rules and we feel more free and natural. I have discovered so many different places and met so many wonderful people from trail running. Second, I met my wife Annie in that first race, which brought me here to France and eventually to UTMB.

By the first UTMB, I'd been running in the Alps for a few years, but had never run more than 70K. I really wasn't sure that I could make the full lap, but was excited to see how far I could go. We left at 4:00 a.m like a small family heading out, but after the Col du Bonhomme, I ran alone for the rest of the race. At Courmayeur, I wasn't tired so I decided to continue on to Champex-Lac. I was told that the second place person was an hour behind me. I stayed for 30 minutes, ate two bowls of pasta, and got a massage before leaving quietly to head back to Chamonix.

Everyone remembers the bad weather during that first year at UTMB, but I enjoyed the storm. If I have a choice between sun and cold, I'll take the cold. The fresh weather gives me energy. I was worried about the other runners still out in those terrifying conditions though.

At the finish it was midnight and pouring rain, but all the Chamonix kids came out to run with me. There were probably 100 people waiting for my arrival under umbrellas. It was the first race I had ever won and was a really special experience. Karla [Valladares] came out in the rain and gave me a hug, even though we barely knew each other.

My life now is a little quieter. I work for the city of Geneva at the Metro. I stopped competing in ultra distances in 2010, but trail running is still a big part of my life. Annie and I spend a lot of time doing humanitarian work and organizing our expedition races in Tibet, Nepal, India, and Indonesia with Dawa Sherpa Experiences. The races help support my association, Godfathers and Godmothers for Nepal, which looks after children and the elderly in remote villages of the Everest valley.

Annie and I also love to garden. In the summertime, I spend a lot of time outside, growing every vegetable possible from potatoes and pumpkins to lettuce. I don't buy any vegetables at the supermarket and I love being able to give them away in my village.

FRANÇOIS D'HAENE: "IT'S PERSONAL BETWEEN YOU AND THE MOUNTAIN"

Four-time UTMB winner François D'Haene shares some of his favorite UTMB memories from across the years. From star-gazing on the trail to holding his family close at the finish, D'Haene says that even with all the crowds and all the buzz, UTMB can still offer deeply personal, emotional moments.

I discovered UTMB as a physiotherapy student in 2004. I was there as a volunteer giving massages, so I could practice and improve. I had been running for about 10 years, but when I saw the big loop on the map, I thought "Wow, in one day? This challenge is crazy!" And so I went back home and signed up for CCC with my father. I ran that event for a couple of years until I was 20 and was old enough that I could run UTMB.

I have run UTMB five times now and have wonderful memories from each edition. In 2011, I didn't finish. When I stopped, I realized my mistake was not during the race, but during my preparation. This race is just a sport. I needed to remember that. There must be pleasure in it, too. So I said, "Okay, I will go again in 2012, but with less pressure and better training—more days in the mountains with friends." From then on, I always think about that approach.

In 2012, it was my first time running for Salomon. Kilian had gone to run another race and the team managers let me know they were really counting on me. It was very important for me to do well for the team. When I finished it was five in the morning, raining, and no one was there to see me win except my team and my family. It was a bit emotional for me, even more than the way it is now at the finish line, with tons of people.

The next time, in 2014, I won again and my wife and youngest daughter were at the finish, waiting. I picked up my daughter and crossed the finish line with her. My fa-

ther was also running that year. When he crossed, we were all waiting for him and he also took my daughter across the finish line. When I got home and saw the picture of her crossing with both dad and grandpa in the same year... it was just, "Wow."

In 2017, I remember the honorable competition among the first ten or 15 runners. Not a lot of us dropped out. Everyone was focused on the challenge more than the competition, not pushing too much and running very smartly. We were not fighting each other, however. We understood that it's personal between you and the mountain.

And finally in 2021, yes, I won again. But what I really remember is my wife and three kids at the finish. When your small kids look at you and they push you, literally, right to the finish—it's crazy. There were maybe 10,000 people around us cheering the runners, but for that 30 seconds, I forgot everybody and it was just the five of us. For me, to finish like that, well, it was a very emotional thing.

UTMB is very popular, which makes it special in its own way, but you can also still find some solitude. It's not too long out of Chamonix that you're alone on the trail and soon, you join the night. You can feel the stars in the sky. It's the best part for me. Even when the trail is busy, you are still sharing special moments, like stars and sunrises, with fellow runners. Those moments, and sharing the finish lines with my family, they're some of my favorite memories.

During the 2008 edition of UTMB, word started to spread along the course that a young Catalan runner was hanging tight with three other race leaders. The twenty-year-old runner was racing without a trail-running vest, seemingly ignoring the required equipment list.

Was this young phenom bending the rules? Not really. "He was clearly within the rules," remembered Catherine Poletti when I asked her about it. "He just knew the rules very precisely." Poletti had inspected the runner's gear herself. He ran with a tiny jacket that had the zippers cut off, and a survival blanket that was about 10 centimeters square. "I asked him, 'What do you think you will protect with that?!'"

Today, Catherine Poletti laughs about the experience. Back in 2008, however, the race organization quickly learned their lesson. The following year's race regulations were much more exacting. (See required gear list, page 92)

The young runner out front was Kilian Jornet, from Cerdanya, Spain. Jornet's sister, Naila, cheering on her brother near the Swiss-Italian border, added some context for confused onlookers. "He's a ski mountaineering champion. He just carries what he needs, and that's all."

The gear was tucked neatly under Jornet's shirt. Along the course, athlete managers from other brands complained. Just what was going on? Race marshals along the course checked Jornet's equipment no fewer than eight times.

But at Col Montets, about 17 kilometers from the finish, an issue arose that remains a point of contention to this day. The UTMB organization said two or three runners paced Jornet, starting around Col Montets. (Pacers, runners who help set a steady speed for a competitor, are not allowed at UTMB.) Jornet remembers it differently. "It was some spectator that started running with me," he told me.

At Tête aux Vents, UTMB hit Jornet with a 15-minute penalty and went through all his gear again.

Jornet was deflated. "At that point, I wanted to quit the race," he told me. He was on the verge of dropping. "I was happy with my race to that point," he said. In the end, he ran the final high balcony traverse, and the downhill to the finish line in Chamonix. "I was like, 'Okay, I need to just finish'. I enjoyed the finish line."

"Kilian Jornet is someone who respects the rules," said Catherine Poletti. "We can absolutely say it was not his idea." "But in this case," added Michel Poletti, "he needed to be more careful. He needed to tell those runners, 'You need to go away.'"

What is clear is that, even many years later, no one is very happy with how events transpired that day. "It was still the early years of the race," said Michel Poletti. "We were obliged to [set a standard showing that] the rules are the rules."

"He's a good guy," stressed Catherine Poletti fourteen years later. "All during those controls, he was smiling and very Zen. No stress. He showed everything. Maybe sometimes we haven't agreed," she added. "But I respect his capacity to do exactly what he thinks is right and to follow exactly what he thinks and to adapt to the moment."

REQUIRED GEAR LIST

MATERIALS

BAG OR VEST
Must carry the required equipment during the race.

PERSONAL CUP
150 milliliters minimum. Cannot be a bottle or flask.

2 HEADLAMPS OR FLASHLIGHTS
Recommended 200+ lumens for the main lamp. Spare cells/batteries.

IDENTITY DOCUMENT
Any official document to prove your identity, like a passport.

SECURITY

MOBILE PHONE
Must stay on and work in the three countries.

WHISTLE
In case you're out of sight of other runners and need help.

SELF ADHESIVE ELASTIC BANDAGE
Minimum 100x6 cm for a bandage or strapping.

SURVIVAL BLANKET
Must be at least 1.40m x 2m.

NUTRITION AND HYDRATION

SUPPLY OF WATER
Must have a minimum capacity of 1 liter.

FOOD RESERVE
Recommended 800 kcal. E.g., 2 gels and 2 energy bars.

CLOTHING

JACKET WITH HOOD
With sealed seams and specific requirements for waterproofing and breathability.

ADDITIONAL WARM SECOND LAYER
Non-cotton long sleeve layer with specific weight requirements.

CAP
Warm hat or fleece buff® to protect from the cold.

CAP OR BANDANA OR BUFF®
Head covering to protect from warm, sunny conditions.

LONG-LEGGED PANTS OR RACE LEGGINGS
Or combination of leggings and socks which cover the legs.

WATERPROOF OVERPANTS
To wear over pants or race leggings in wet weather.

GLOVES
Warm and waterproof gloves, or gloves with waterproof over glove.

HOT WEATHER KIT (IN YEARS OF HOT WEATHER)

SUNGLASSES

SAHARAN CAP
Or any combination that fully covers the head and neck.

SUNSCREEN CREAM
To protect against sunburn in sunny conditions.

MINIMUM WATER
Supply 2 liters instead of the standard 1 liter.

COLD WEATHER KIT

3RD WARM LAYER
Intermediary layer between the 2nd layer and the waterproof jacket.

ROBUST AND CLOSED TRAIL-RUNNING SHOES
Minimalist or ultralight running shoes are not allowed.

It was, perhaps, a learning moment for both Jornet and UTMB. Just like trail running itself, he too was growing up, and fast. In many ways, UTMB and Jornet—though so very different in their aspirations—traveled a similar trajectory. They had both come into trail running at the perfect moment. The sport was just about to explode.

At the finish that day, Jornet was filled with mixed emotions. "I was happy about how I was racing. But from Tête Aux Vents, I just wanted to get it finished and go home," Jornet told me.

UTMB in 2008 was a sort of foreshadowing in another way, too. At the front of the pack during much of the first half of the race was a runner named Nico Mermoud. Mermoud had placed third in the prior year's UTMB, and in 2008 he was beginning to explore a new design for a trail running shoe, one that reduced fatigue and allowed runners to go faster downhill. Later that year, he formed a new company with partner Jean-Luc Diard. To name it, they picked a phrase from the Māori language, pronounced *hoh-kuh onay onay*, meaning "fly over the earth." The name would later be abbreviated to, simply, Hoka.

A KITCHEN-TABLE OFFICE

UTMB in those nascent days was literally a home-grown business. Catherine worked in the living room of the Polettis' house in Chamonix. During these early years of UTMB, it was just Catherine at the helm—one of the few female race directors globally. Though she rarely points it out publicly, she became a sort of accidental pioneer. Poletti's role is often overlooked by critics who would like to see the race doing more for women. For her part, Poletti also notes that she was not a trail runner, either. "My knowledge of trail running was that of someone who had accompanied and assisted her husband on many races. I would often joke with Michel that I knew more runners, more families of runners and more aspects of the race than he did. He knew those who went at his speed, whereas I had the opportunity to meet the volunteers, the families of the runners and the runners who went faster than Michel." That mix of trail runner and supporter would go on to be a good combination for the couple.

Catherine's wonderfully low-key home office scene was all about to change, and quickly.

The wheels had been put in motion the moment Karla Valladares came to Chamonix in 2003, bringing UTMB a sponsor from the outset: The North Face (see Karla Valladares memory of the day on page 48). That serendipity also gave the Polettis an influential champion and a lasting friend—Topher Gaylord. Managing Director, EMEA (Europe, Middle East, Africa) for The North Face and an ultrarunner for some years already, Gaylord had been casting about for a 100-mile race in Europe to run himself. He'd signed up for the first edition of UTMB. Though no one could predict it at the time, the partnership with The North Face would last a decade, and Gaylord and Karla Valladares would become key players in the race around Mont Blanc through to the present day.

Gaylord felt an immediate and authentic connection with the Polettis. "UTMB was something that would fortify our friendship for years to come," he said. And in the race, he saw something that might overcome the fragmentation of the European market that was a challenge for The North Face. "It was a great way for us to have a pan-European event. UTMB is a universal language of adventure."

Gaylord and his team ended up working closely with UTMB for many years, planning each year's race and going to press conferences. Gaylord and Michel Poletti would run along the trails around Mont Blanc, dreaming up new ideas for the race. In time, it became a tradition. "It's a religion for us now," Gaylord said.

Through UTMB's later partnerships, Gaylord remained one of Poletti's closest friends. "We're bonded," he once said. "We have a friendship that outlasts brands." And so it was, with Gaylord's enthusiasm and the key North Face partnership, that two years after the launch of UTMB, when the organization had a little more money, it added its first office—a tiny chalet-style cabin called a mazot that the team built from a kit. The building still sits in the family's yard. "We told the interns that summer, 'Your first job is to build your office!'" It was 16 square meters but a huge improvement over the living room and kitchen.

Sixteen square meters might have seemed spacious at the time, but a lot more would soon be needed. In 2009, US author Christopher McDougall, a foreign correspondent for the Associated Press, would write *Born to Run*. The story of Mexico's ultramarathon running Tarahumara tribe would go on to become the top-selling running book of all time, spending four months on the *New York Times* bestseller list and selling more than three million copies. With a lively cast of long-distance trail runners, McDougall's writing brought the niche sport of trail running to the world's attention.

Back in the US, Bob Crowley, a technology entrepreneur and private equity investor who later served as president of the International Trail Running Association, was experiencing the wave firsthand. In 1995, he was an early member of Trail Animals Running Club, a New England–based club with a paper newsletter that was mailed out to its 30 members. "It was mostly road runners who fueled the growth," said Crowley, who explained that road running had become too serious, too race-focused. "They were looking to run for fun, for release, and to stay in shape." The new world wide web allowed disillusioned road runners to discover trail running groups in their vicinity. Today, TARC is one of the largest trail-running clubs in the world, with over seven thousand online followers.

Over at the trail race registration website Ultrasignup, software developer Mark Gilligan was watching something remarkable happen. Between 2003 and 2010, the number of races on his homegrown registration platform grew by 164%. Substantial as it was, this was just the beginning. By 2022, the number of races on Ultrasignup had grown by 1,143%.

By and large, the story was the same the world over. In 2002, the year before the first UTMB, the German ultrarunning association Deutsche Ultramarathon Vereinigung recorded 47,470 unique ultramarathon finishers. By 2019, that number had burgeoned nearly ninefold, to 430,652.

It all made a certain amount of sense. Trail running might be one of humanity's oldest sports, but it is also perfect for the twenty-first century. Purists love its simplicity—runner, shoes, trail—and many people feel the need for an escape from the ever louder noise of modern life. It is also tailor-made for social media, and the solitary sport has become a shared passion on Facebook, Strava, and Instagram, where stunning shots of runners in dramatic places are so exquisitely shareable.

UTMB, set in Europe's epic mountain playground, was the perfect fit, and its numbers grew in parallel with these developments. In 2006, the race filled up in three weeks; in 2007, it took just ten hours. And in 2008? The race filled in nine minutes. A year later, a lottery system was ready but not needed, as UTMB had established entry requirements, asking runners to show they had run either two 50-kilometer runs or one 80-kilometer race. That year, the race accepted all 2,648 runners who signed up. Finally, in 2010, with the numbers still increasing, the lottery kicked in.

The growth in the sport was fortuitous for the Polettis, who already had ambitions as large as the swelling numbers of trail runners, thanks to their experience at Vasaloppet, a Nordic ski race in Sweden. When they first went to Vasaloppet, three decades ago, it was a single race. A decade later, during their last visit, it had mushroomed to eight events with ten thousand skiers and supporters. Vasaloppet now spanned an entire week. "It was fun. Vasaloppet became a model for us," Michel Poletti told me. "We wanted to have a big party around Mont Blanc."

Starting in 2006, UTMB added a dizzying array of races, each with its own acronym: CCC ("Courmayeur-Champex-Chamonix"), TDS ("Sur les Traces des Ducs de Savoie"), OCC ("Orsières - Champex - Chamonix"), and finally PTL ("La Petite Trotte à Léon"). Each race filled a niche: the 100-kilometer CCC was designed to be more accessible than the UTMB. The TDS, originally 119 kilometers and now 145, was created to explore the wild Beaufortain region not far from Chamonix. The 55-kilometer OCC brought a race start to Switzerland and offered a shorter course.

Finally, in 2008, the organization added a massive 300-kilometer event called the Petite Trotte à Léon (PTL), teasingly named for Léon Lovey, the pastry chef in Champex-Lac who served as lead organizer for the Swiss portion of UTMB. The creation of PTL was an effort to bring back some of the original sense of adventure from the early days of UTMB. "People were telling us UTMB was getting too commercial," said Catherine Poletti. "We wanted something a bit more committing, with the spirit of a team in the mountains, almost like a rope team."

It could be said that by 2008, with the start of the PTL, UTMB had grown up: the dream of a Vasaloppet-style event around Mont Blanc had been achieved, and the race formats stayed largely unchanged for more than a dozen years. As the race grew and grew and grew, chatter started. Was there a point at which UTMB would become simply too large for the good of trail running? "There's been a lot of conversation around UTMB getting too big," said Topher Gaylord. "The reality is trail running is the fastest growing segment of the running market and running is the largest participation sport in the world today. And trail running races are exploding around the world."

UTMB had changed by 2008. So, too, had the runners. Kilian Jornet might have raised eyebrows with his gear, but he was there to win. From seemingly out of nowhere, the twenty-year-old runner from Catalonia went on to beat Dawa Sherpa by an hour and six seconds. If ever there was a sign that trail running was changing, this was it.

THE ULTRA-TERRESTRIAL

Kilian Jornet was creating the swell—and surfing it, too, winning races around the globe as he became a household name for trail runners everywhere. Jornet dominated the highly technical world of skyrunning, a vertiginous sport that borrowed from both alpinism and trail running. He was winning on less airy courses, too. At Switzerland's Sierre-Zinal, a 31-kilometer affair that some consider to be the world's most competitive shorter-distance trail race, he stood atop the podium a record nine times, and in 2019 broke a sixteen-year-old course record that had been set by the legendary New Zealand runner, Jonathan Wyatt.

In short, Jornet became trail running's first superstar. In many ways, he was and continues to be the perfect ambassador for the sport: humble and introverted, passionate about the values of trail running, reluctant to be in the spotlight, and eager to acknowledge the accomplishments of others. An early sponsorship with Salomon grew into a deep and symbiotic relationship. For years, Jornet was the face of the brand's top-of-the-line S/Lab shoes, and the French brand produced online films and social media starring him. In 2013, the *New York Times* featured a piece on Jornet called "Becoming the All-Terrain Human." Though still young, he had already won more than eighty races. In Europe, he was nicknamed "L'ultra-terrestre," a French word mélange suggesting he was one part extraterrestrial and one-part ultrarunner and yet also keenly in touch with the ground ("terre"). His contracts with Salomon grew into six figures, something incomprehensible to the previous generation of trail runners.

In 2010, Jornet moved to Chamonix, which was quickly becoming the place to be not only for alpinism but for trail running as well. He climbed, skied, and ran hard. On July 11, 2013, at age twenty-five, he set out to break a record: to run and then climb from the steps of the Saint Michel Church—the start zone for UTMB—up and then down Mont Blanc. Strong mountain athletes are happy to complete the route in under 24 hours. "Snow conditions were good," he modestly told France TV at the time. "As a result, I could slide on my rear [on parts of the way down] and run." He completed the ascent and descent of the Alps' highest peak in 4 hours 57 minutes and 44 seconds. The record still stands today. The "Fastest Known Time," or "FKT," up and down Mont Blanc was part of a larger project Jornet had dreamed up and called "Summits of My Life," which involved setting speed records around the world—including on Mount Everest, whose north face he climbed without supplemental oxygen or the use of fixed ropes, leaving the base camp at 17,600 feet on a Saturday evening at 10 p.m. and reaching the top of the world, at 29,031 feet, around midnight on Sunday.

LET'S TALK ABOUT BIBS

In addition to the information on the front of the bib, each runner is provided with two electronic chips (one on the back of the bib and one attached the the runner's bag). The chips are read by timing mats and handheld readers to track runners' progress.

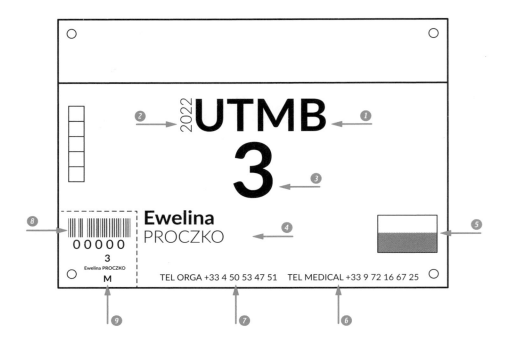

1. Name of the race: Identifies which race the runner is competing in. The text color also corresponds to that specific race.
2. Race year.
3. Bib number: The unique number identifier for every runner.
4. Runner name: The runner's full name.
5. Nationality flag: Shows the flag of the nationality of the runner.
6. Medical number: The number runners should call if there is a medical emergency on the course.
7. Organization number: The number runners should call if they have any non-medical questions during the race.
8. The bar code offers another unique way for UTMB to identify the runner and their race, for tracking each runner, recording their location if they drop out, and awarding finisher prizes.
9. T-shirt size.

Meanwhile, Chamonix had become to the outdoors world what Cannes was for films, and the endless attention and climbing one-up-manship simply became too much for Jornet. In 2015, he and his partner Emelie Forsberg moved to a quiet valley in Norway. But Jornet was not done with UTMB, which he won again in 2009 and 2011. And there was more to come.

In 2014, UTMB took its first official step onto the global trail-running stage, bringing together ten of the world's top ultra-races to form the Ultra-Trail World Tour. The Tour was the next step in a dream that had taken shape in the Polettis' minds around 2005; by the time it ended in 2021, it had grown to include several dozen races.

When the Polettis talk about the genesis of this global network of trail races, one sees exactly what drove them. "It's a question of passion, and it's also a question of esprit d'entreprise," said Michel Poletti when I interviewed him in the fall of 2022, mixing languages to find the best way to describe the business drive he and Catherine share.

Here, Poletti paused, reflecting, and in one fell swoop captured the arc of UTMB and the motivating factors in a single paragraph:

From the beginning, we wanted to develop it to become a great event. Did we have ambitious plans for the race? Yes. But UTMB has become greater than we could have imagined in 2003. In 2004 we saw it would become a great event, and we also saw other big events in the world. We had more runners coming to UTMB from overseas, and we understood that something would happen internationally. [Modern] trail running was born in the US, but in Europe it was exploding. We already had the example of a week-long series of races that existed in Nordic skiing. And so, it became our dream to make UTMB part of what we saw as a beautiful international movement.

One part passion, one part entrepreneurial spirit.

But someone beat them to it.

In 2012, a group called the International Skyrunning Federation (ISF) in nearby Biella, Italy, which had focused on daring, technical races that included sections of trail in alpine environments, launched a new circuit of races. But something caught the attention of the Polettis. "These were trail races, not true skyraces," Michel Poletti said. Skyrunning had defined itself as technical races that went over 2,000 meters, and several races in the new series, such as Transvulcania and Templiers, are to this day considered traditional trail races. A year later, Skyrunning added another comparatively non-technical race, the Marathon Mont Blanc.

"We thought this bringing together of races was a brilliant idea," said Poletti. But the organization had made an interesting choice. "Their ultra races were all no more than about 70 km," he said. "We thought, 'Wow.' We had wanted to launch an international series, but they did it first. We had to give them credit for that." The following year, Skyrunning announced an international series of 100-km races. "We said, 'No way!' These ultra trail races are exactly what we do."

The two organizations had been thinking along parallel lines. "At the same time, we were thinking it was time to work on our dream of gathering the best ultra races in the world together." Thus was born the Ul-tra-Trail World Tour. To those deep in the trail running world, the future was taking shape. But who would be part of the next chapter? That was unclear.

In Poletti's mind, there was yet another issue that was wrong. Sky-running's announcement of the new series also said that the organization would be the International Federation for trail running. "They called themselves a federation, but they had a private race series. I thought it was unclear. It wasn't a true federation. There's a place in the sport for a federation and a place for private companies."

In answer, Poletti drove the creation of ITRA, the International Trail Running Association. "I thought it could become the true governing body of trail running, and Ultra-Trail World Tour would be the private side of long distance trail running."

In one year, two new trail running organizations were created. But the Ultra-Trail World Tour was hobbled from the outset. The connections between the events were weak, with different rules, sponsors, and spirit. For the runners, the "UTWT" experience varied wildly. "Everything was different from race to race," said Catherine Poletti. Nor was it a sustainable model, financially. "The fees from the races were not enough to cover the costs of managing the tour," said Michel Poletti. "We were losing money."

The organization needed something new, but it wasn't clear just what, yet. It would take the arrival of an ambitious sports entrepreneur, Rémi Duchemin, to crystalize that vision.

WHO IS THIS BUSINESSMAN FROM PARIS?

Though UTMB was growing on the outside, behind the scenes it was still very much in its infancy. "You have a jewel here, but it's very fragile," Rémi Duchemin told the organization in 2013. Duchemin, who was CEO of the Swiss marketing company OC Sport, was a close friend of the Polettis. They had met seven years earlier, when Duchemin was exploring new op-portunities for his then-employer, ASO, the organizer of Tour de France.

"At the time, I think they thought, 'Who is this businessman from Paris?'" said Duchemin. Over the years, however, Duchemin became a trusted advisor. He took part in UTMB races, and in the off-season, he and the Polettis visited each other. "Ninety-nine percent of the conversation," Duchemin recalls, "was about UTMB or trail running. I always thought, 'One day, we will do something together.'"

In early 2016, Michel Poletti and Duchemin went ski touring togeth-er, high above Switzerland's Rhône valley. "Our dream," Poletti said to Duchemin, "is to have a major trail-running race in San Francisco." The Bay Area, one of the trail-running hotspots in the US, had developed a lively community devoted to the sport.

"I said, 'OK, let's make it happen,'" remembers Duchemin. He got to work, traveling around the world talking to potential partners, pitching the idea of UTMB international races. The organization, with its growing media power and expertise, would provide guidance and oversight and

leverage its global audience. For two years, Duchemin knocked on doors from Asia to the US, signing early deals for races in China and Oman, and on April 28, 2017, UTMB and OC Sport announced a global series of UTMB-licensed trail races.

It was a huge leap forward in the business of UTMB, and for once, Michel Poletti was skeptical. Would UTMB resonate with a global audience, and so much so that race promoters would pay the necessary six figures for a franchise? UTMB was charging franchise fees that were twice what The North Face was paying to sponsor the race in Chamonix.

The Bay Area race never came to fruition, but many others did, and by 2021, the new company had grown to include franchised races around the world, including events in China, Oman, Argentina, Spain, and Thailand, with all the races building towards the UTMB at the end of August in Chamonix. From Duchemin's point of view, this was the right direction—growth coupled with the resilience of multiple venues around the world, at different times of the year.

But from a business point of view, there was a hitch. "It was the first time I had created a company without having the full vision right at the start," Duchemin said. "That came two years later. From day one, the Polettis made it crystal clear that the door was closed to being acquired." UTMB was and always will be a family business, the Polettis told Duchemin, foreshadowing later conversations with other prospective partners.

That they would leave UTMB to the next generation was always clear in the Polettis' mind. "It continues to be a strong motivation for Catherine and Michel," said Duchemin.

Even with the ink drying on international deals, UTMB remained something less than an established multinational company. "Some people in the running community like to think that Michel and Catherine have made a fortune," Duchemin told me. "But it's totally false."

When Duchemin studied the accounts, he was surprised by what he found. "In a good year, the company never made more than 25,000 euros, net," he said. "In a bad year, it was a loss." Long ago, the Polettis had made a pivotal decision. "They decided to reinvest everything into the development of the race," said Duchemin. "It's why UTMB is such a big event today—they put all the money back into infrastructure and communication platforms." The businessman in Duchemin was taken aback. "Looking at the statements, the financial reserves were small. It wasn't good."

Throughout this period, Duchemin brought a new level of strategic thinking to the enterprise. He worked on adding reserves and building a stronger financial base. In September 2018, he implemented a plan that helped carry out his dream, placing all the UTMB assets in one new business, called the UTMB Group. The Group included the UTMB International; LiveTrail, an associated trail race IT company that also provided its services to other events around the world; the still extant Ultra-Trail World Tour; and, of course, the original UTMB Mont Blanc.

Major multinational sports marketing companies with long track records were dipping their toes into the trail running world. UTMB needed a rainy-day fund, and the business might want to diversify. Or, as Duchemin pointed out at the time, with a prescience that was downright eerie, "There might be a crisis of some kind."

BIG BUSINESS SETS ITS EYES ON TRAIL RUNNING

By 2018, Duchemin had seen that trail running was changing. "Trail running wasn't a niche sport anymore," he said. "It wasn't a mass sport, either, but we saw that could happen in ten years' time." In his mind, the time was right for investing. "If we had invested five years earlier, it would have been too risky. Five years later, and it would have been too late."

The data backed him up. Global trail running shoes were a billion-dollar market in 2015. By 2025, by some analyses, it will have grown to several times that size. UTMB itself was experiencing this surge, too: registration demand increased nearly 70% between 2016 and 2019. World Athletics, the world's governing body for track and field events, estimates that there are twenty million trail runners worldwide, that the sport is growing at a rate of 15% a year, and that the trend will continue. And Krissy Moehl, the women's winner of the first UTMB? She was now a race director herself, in the Pacific Northwest of the United States. Her race, the Chuckanut 50, started as a local event with twenty-six finishers in 1995. By 2022, that number had ballooned to 430.

Major players started courting UTMB. "They were all looking at UTMB. It was a logical place to start. In a window of twelve months, we met with everyone," said Duchemin. The Polettis and Duchemin had discussions with Spartan, Ironman, Virgin Sports, Motiv Sports, and ASO, owners of the Tour du France. Each group of well-heeled visitors to Chamonix tried for an acquisition, but Michel and Catherine never wanted to sell. To every offer, the Polettis said, "No thanks."

"But we knew that these players, with big pockets, were trying to get into trail running," said Duchemin. Without a strong financial partner, Duchemin was worried the race would be in big trouble if a downturn arrived. Financing would dry up, and they'd be forced to sell to a partner that didn't share their goals and values—in other words, to a company that was just interested in trail running for the cash it could spin off for shareholders. UTMB was at risk. At this point, Duchemin turned to Groupe Télégramme, a major French media group that was already part-owner of OC Sport. The family-owned company, which only made long-term investments, was very much in the spirit of UTMB, and in the spring of 2019 acquired 40% of UTMB through a capital increase, in which proceeds went directly to the company. "It was reassuring for Catherine and Michel," said Duchemin. Over the years, casual onlookers have wondered if the Polettis pocketed income during this sale. To that, Michel Poletti has a simple answer. "Not one euro. It all was invested in the company."

A strong foundation. Corporate governance. All the assets under one entity. And during this time, a long-term goal came into clearer focus: to pass the company down to the next generation—namely, to David and Isabelle. UTMB had become a totally new company, ready to face an uncertain new era in trail running—one that, for better or worse, now

UTMB MONT-BLANC SERIES
DEVELOPMENT OVER TIME

The UTMB event in August has continued to grow and add more race distances over the years.

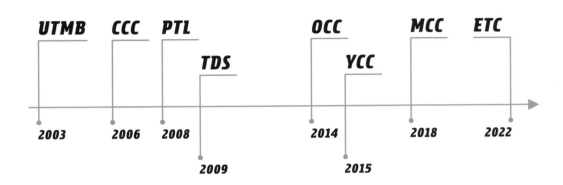

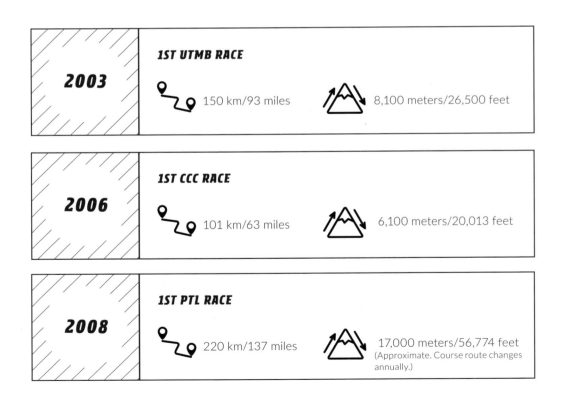

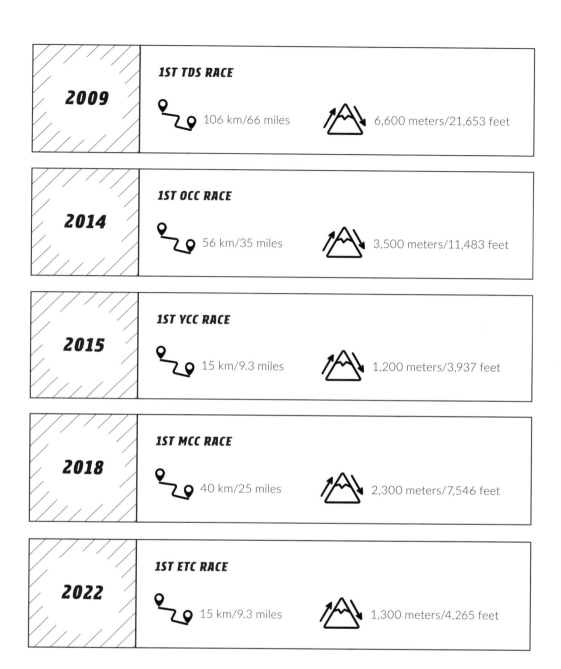

2009

1ST TDS RACE

106 km/66 miles   6,600 meters/21,653 feet

2014

1ST OCC RACE

56 km/35 miles   3,500 meters/11,483 feet

2015

1ST YCC RACE

15 km/9.3 miles   1,200 meters/3,937 feet

2018

1ST MCC RACE

40 km/25 miles   2,300 meters/7,546 feet

2022

1ST ETC RACE

15 km/9.3 miles   1,300 meters/4,265 feet

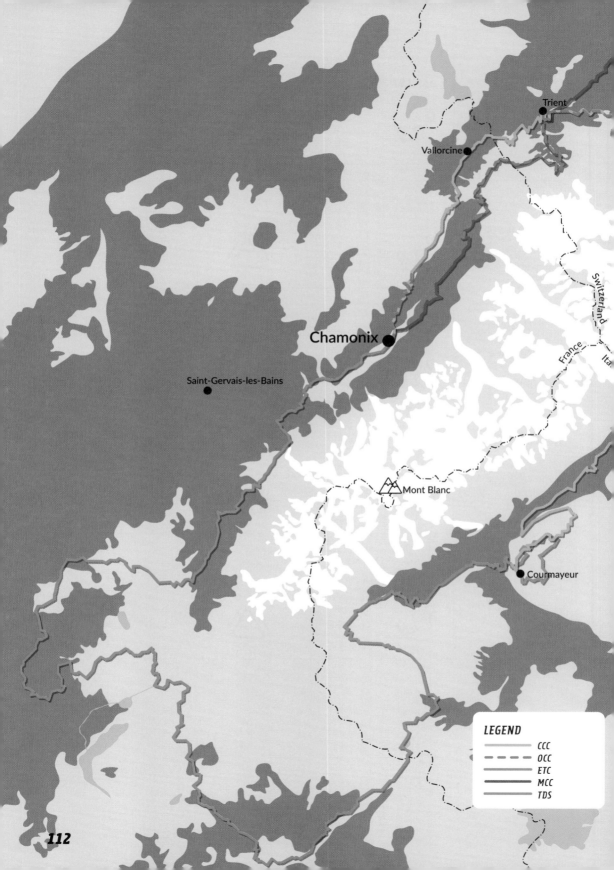

Trient

Vallorcine

Chamonix

Saint-Gervais-les-Bains

Switzerland

France

Ita

Mont Blanc

Courmayeur

LEGEND

CCC
OCC
ETC
MCC
TDS

Orsières

La Fouly

included big business. Through 2019, everything went according to plan.

What could go wrong? On February 8, 2020, the Polettis, along with everyone else in the Chamonix valley, picked up their copies of *Le Dauphine*, the regional newspaper. Five cases of a novel virus from Wuhan, China had shown up in a holiday chalet in nearby Les Contamines. At noon on March 17, France went into the first of three national lockdowns.

Suddenly, the world changed, and with it, trail running as well. UTMB's international races were all canceled, save for a race in Thailand. Eighty percent of the Ultra-Trail World Tour races were canceled.

The Chamonix races were canceled, too. That summer, the normally bustling mountain city was a ghost town.

"Very quickly," said Duchemin, "we realized that we had a tough choice: either we had to lay off 70% of the staff, or we had to use all of our new financial reserves." The Polettis and Duchemin chose to keep the staff engaged, but it cost them dearly.

"We lost 1.5 million euros in one year," said Duchemin. "Thank God we had those reserves."

THE SUITS ARRIVE IN CHAMONIX

Over the years since that first flurry of interest, the courting had continued unabated from one company in particular: the Ironman Group. The sports marketing company based in Tampa, Florida, had developed triathlons into a global phenomenon, and it had paid off handsomely. The company was worth more than 700 million dollars. But the sport had peaked in the US in 2015 and since then had been steadily declining, and the Ironman Group was casting about for the next big thing. (In this book we refer to the IRONMAN Group by the name 'Ironman' for sake of readability. This should not be confused with Ironman triathalons.)

The only reason Ironman even had trail running on its radar was thanks to one run in 2017. Dave Beeche, then a Senior Vice President at Ironman, had gotten acquainted with trail running while taking part in the 100-kilometer Ultra-Trail Australia. "It was like a lightbulb went off for me. I thought it was incredible. The vibe was totally different from any other endurance event. I had great conversations. It was inclusive, not exclusive. It was collaborative, not competitive. I asked for advice and everyone was offering help."

In trail running, Beeche saw a different community from the triathlon world. "There's one bucket of people who just love exploring nature. Trail running is part of the journey for them. They'd never be caught dead in an Ironman," he said at the time. "And there is a group of people who have done Ironmans and are ready for new challenges and new goals."

Ironman liked what they saw. To test the waters, on May 15, 2018, they made a purchase—Ultra-Trail Australia, the first race Beeche ran.

"We started looking at the fundamentals of the trail-running market," Andrew Messick, CEO of Ironman Group, told me just outside the posh Mont Blanc Hotel during UTMB week at the close of August 2022. Just a few dozen meters away, at Place du Triangle de l'Amitié, runners in the UTMB TDS race were crossing the finish line. "It became clear that it was a small and rapidly growing sector. It looked a lot like triathlons looked thirty or forty years ago. That is, relatively small, led by highly passionate people, and highly fragmented. UTMB feels a lot like Kona [the Ironman World Championship, held in Kailua-Kona, Hawaii]. You have a sense that you are exactly in the center of the sport's universe."

"This trend feels sustained, authentic, and long-term to me," said Beeche. "There are many channels to explore in the sport. You can go further, you can go to new countries, or you can just try to do better in your local race. It doesn't feel like a color run to me," he said, referencing the road-running fad where participants were sprayed with a new color each kilometer for 5 kilometers.

In Ironman, there was suddenly a player at the table who was working hard to develop trail racing internationally. But to cover costs and keep shareholders happy, Ironman had to push. "The financials of trail-running races get interesting around two thousand participants," said Beeche. "That's your rough benchmark of where you can make a profit. And when you get to five thousand, you're making some good money. The participation numbers are the engine room of the business. That's what's driving it all." How does a company like Ironman profit from those numbers? Merchandise is a big part of the story. "The zealots turn their noses up at merchandise, but did you see the merch tent at UTMB?" Beeche has a point. When I visited in August 2022, the tents and booths spread across the area the size of a soccer field were packed. "There's a philosophical question there, of course," Beeche pointed out. "I'm environmentally conscious. But there's demand there that UTMB is meeting."

Others have been a little more blunt about it. "It's about the cheap beer, the cold pizza, and the high entry fees," said Barry Siff. In 2009, Siff sold eight Colorado triathlons to Ironman. He has also served as President of USA Triathlon. "That's their formula. You have to have the numbers. When all is said and done, it all relates to profitability."

Ironman knew they wanted into trail running, and UTMB was the perfect venue to own. But there was just one small problem.

"We had told them we were not for sale," Duchemin told me. That didn't stop Messick, though. Several times a year, he and Matthieu Van Veen, Ironman's Chief Revenue Officer, would come to Chamonix, organize dinners, and try to get traction with UTMB for a deal.

When the Polettis were considering partners for UTMB, at least one well-heeled brand was shown the door because of its lack of alignment on values. "I do not think," Michel Poletti said, and then took a long pause, picking his words with precision, "that Spartan shares our values." Speaking off the record, several people in the trail running world with first-hand knowledge of the obstacle race company have expanded on Poletti's circumspect comment. They describe a corporate culture at Spartan that was aggressive and often at odds with the community vibe that dominates trail running. "They're commandos," one person told me. "It's all about combat, on and off the trail." (When I reached out to Spartan, they declined to comment.)

UTMB WINNERS 2003-2022

Year	Name	Country	Time
	MEN		
2003	Dachhiri-Dawa Sherpa	Nepal	20:05:58
2004	Vincent Delebarre	France	21:06:18
2005	Christophe Jaquerod	Switzerland	21:11:07
2006	Marco Olmo	Italy	21:06:06 ⭐
2007	Marco Olmo	Italy	21:31:58
2008	Kilian Jornet Burgada	Spain	20:56:59 ⭐
2009	Kilian Jornet Burgada	Spain	21:33:18
2010	Jez Bragg (Altered course)	UK	10:30
2011	Kilian Jornet Burgada	Spain	20:36:43 ⭐
2012	François D'Haene (Altered course)	France	10:32:36
2013	Xavier Thévenard	France	20:34:57 ⭐
2014	François D'Haene	France	20:11:44 ⭐
2015	Xavier Thévenard	France	21:09:15
2016	Ludovic Pommeret	France	22:00:02
2017	François D'Haene (Altered course)	France	19:01:54
2018	Xavier Thévenard	France	20:44:16
2019	Pau Capell	Spain	20:19:07
2020	COVID	-	-
2021	François D'Haene	France	20:46:00
2022	Kilian Jornet Burgada	Spain	19:49:30 ⭐

⭐ new record time

WOMEN

Year	Name	Country	Time
2003	Kristin Moehl	USA	29:38:23
2004	Colette Borcard	Switzerland	26:08:54 ⭐
2005	Elisabeth 'Lizzy' Hawker	UK	26:53:51
2006	Karine Herry	France	25:22:20 ⭐
2007	Nikki Kimball	USA	25:23:45
2008	Elisabeth 'Lizzy' Hawker	UK	25:19:41 ⭐
2009	Kristin Moehl	USA	24:56:01 ⭐
2010	Elisabeth 'Lizzy' Hawker (Altered course)	UK	11:47
2011	Elisabeth 'Lizzy' Hawker	UK	25:02:00
2012	Elisabeth 'Lizzy' Hawker (Altered course)	UK	12:32:13
2013	Rory Bosio	USA	22:37:26 ⭐
2014	Rory Bosio	USA	23:23:20
2015	Nathalie Mauclair	France	25:15:33
2016	Caroline Chaverot	France	25:15:40
2017	Núria Picas (Altered course)	Spain	25:46:43
2018	Francesca Canepa	Italy	26:03:48
2019	Courtney Dauwalter	USA	24:34:26
2020	COVID	-	-
2021	Courtney Dauwalter	USA	22:30:55 ⭐
2022	Katie Schide	USA	23:15:12

"In Ironman," said Poletti, "we found businessmen—and let's be clear, they are businessmen—who were making a lot of money but were honestly open to the values of trail running. We thought we could do business with them and not lose our link to the values we first wrote about in 2003."

Even so, the Polettis rejected offers from Ironman three times. "You can keep coming to Chamonix if you want," Duchemin told Messick once. "It's nice to spend time with you. But the company's not for sale and it will never be. Michel and Catherine will never move a single millimeter from their position."

"If we were only a business, it would have been much simpler. We would have bought a chalet at Les Moussoux and retired," Michel Poletti said, referring to the posh Chamonix neighborhood full of multi-million-dollar chalets a few hundred meters above town.

But by fall 2020, Ironman had shifted their thinking. They were willing to be a minority partner. It was a pretty good match, with Ironman bringing its global understanding of sports business to the table. "We have the commercial network, the marketing ideas, the communications tools," Messick had told the Polettis and Duchemin.

And then there was the matter of the pandemic, still roiling the world and threatening to send UTMB into further financial turmoil. Lockdowns were coming and going in France and around the globe, and the future was uncertain at best. These two factors, according to Duchemin, caused the Polettis to move quickly. They agreed to a partnership.

Duchemin got to work, convincing Groupe Télégramme to sell their shares to Ironman. It wasn't easy. "Télégramme loved UTMB," he said. "And they liked working with the Poletti family." But they finally agreed. Ironman later added another 5% to its minority share of UTMB through a capital increase, still leaving them in a minority position. "Everyone said the Polettis sold the business and made millions, but that's totally wrong," said Duchemin. "Ironman bought their shares from Télégramme."

When the deal was announced on May 6, 2021, the trail-running world exploded in controversy. Many questioned whether Ironman's values really aligned with trail running. John Kelly, a widely respected ultra-marathoner who has participated in eight Ironman ultras, summarized the concerns of many trail runners in a Twitter post that highlighted Ironman's aggressive history: "Monopolization of events through exclusive qualifiers to the "premier" race leading to sky-high entry fees & closure of independent races, complete disregard for host sites, athlete experience & safety, or anything in the way of $, different cultures / goals."

What powered the decision to partner with Ironman? In the end, the new World Series proved pivotal. For UTMB, it took shape during the early months of 2020, and was a curious Covid silver lining. During that time, the Polettis and Rémi Duchemin stepped back to consider their international race series with a fresh perspective. Ultra Trail World Tour, a novel idea when it launched, wasn't working as hoped. "By UTMB," the branded series of races from China to Argentina, launched with an infusion of cash from Group Télégramme, was a confusing intermingling layer.

The pandemic raged. Around the world, companies and individuals

were reevaluating everything. UTMB was not immune to these forces. The Polettis and Duchemin made the decision: scrap the World Tour and start over.

Could everything somehow be unified? It would take cash, and a strong partner, and someone with the skills to help launch a new international race series. It would take someone like, say, Ironman.

At the same time, the Polettis began to realize a sobering fact: Ironman was going to create an international trail race series, with or without UTMB. Did UTMB want to work together, or compete head-to-head? "We knew Ironman was going to go into this space," said Michel Poletti. "They had come into the trail running world quietly, acquiring Ultra-Trail Australia and New Zealand's Tarawera Ultramarathon. They were smart, taking their time." Why not cooperate, instead of a pointless war that would drain resources towards an uncertain outcome?

UTMB called Ironman. At long last, there was a green light. "In the end," Michel Poletti told me, "we decided to build it together instead of fighting against them."

And so, the trail running world got Ironman + UTMB, instead of the two going head-to-head. Which would have benefited the trail running world more? Would Ironman alone have understood trail running's unique culture, or would they have just driven right over it on the way to the bank? It's a moot point, but it's easy to imagine that Ironman without UTMB's deep trail running DNA and obvious passion for the sport might have veered in uncertain directions.

So, UTMB would control all of these races, and to get to run in Chamonix, you would need to collect lottery chances (what UTMB calls "Running Stones") in the World Series races, unless you were an elite runner and could bypass the lottery through top performances at World Series races.

At the 2022 UTMB, Messick quietly took in the scene, dressed not in Ironman clothing but in UTMB gear. "First, trail running is a meeting of friends, and then it is an adventure in nature, and then it is a personal challenge... and only then is it a race," he told me. "And that's the trail ethos. For most runners, times don't matter that much. Those philosophical values are very important in the trail world, and that's quite different from triathlon." A smart answer, but many observers were not going to be placated by Messick's words. They would wait to see what actions followed.

Despite their best efforts, the Poletti family risked losing it all. "We are entrepreneurs and are doing a lot to develop the sport at an international level," Michel told me. "We have to accept the risk of losing control, even if we are doing everything to keep it."

Meanwhile, there had been many other transitions at UTMB. The North Face, with UTMB since the day Topher Gaylord first came to Chamonix on a training run, was shifting its global marketing strategy. The two companies had seemed inextricably linked, but this corporate change ended the partnership. "It was a difficult parting of ways," said Topher Gaylord.

GETTING INTO UTMB MONT-BLANC

There are three ways to get into UTMB Mont-Blanc/UTMB World Series Finals, but the majority of runners will get in through the lottery.

LOTTERY
These are the steps every runner must go through to get into UTMB Mont-Blanc through the lottery.

STEP ONE: GETTING STONES
Runners need at least one "Running Stone" from the past two years and have a valid UTMB Index in the category they want to enter into. UTMB Example: A runner could run a 100-mile or 100-kilometer UTMB World Series event or major in the past 24 months before entering for the lottery. The runner would get either 3 or 4 stones for an event or 6 or 8 stones for a major.

STEP TWO: ENTERING THE LOTTERY
Runners can enter the lottery through the MyUTMB space starting in June of the previous year. The lottery entry (or pre-registration) deadline is 31 December. The number of stones runners have will determine their chances of getting picked in the lottery—the more stones, the higher chances.

STEP THREE: LOTTERY RESULTS
Results for the lottery come out in early January. If picked in the lottery, runners have 10 days to finalize registration by confirming their slot and making the payment.

TRACING ONE RUNNER'S TRACK TO GET INTO UTMB MONT-BLANC

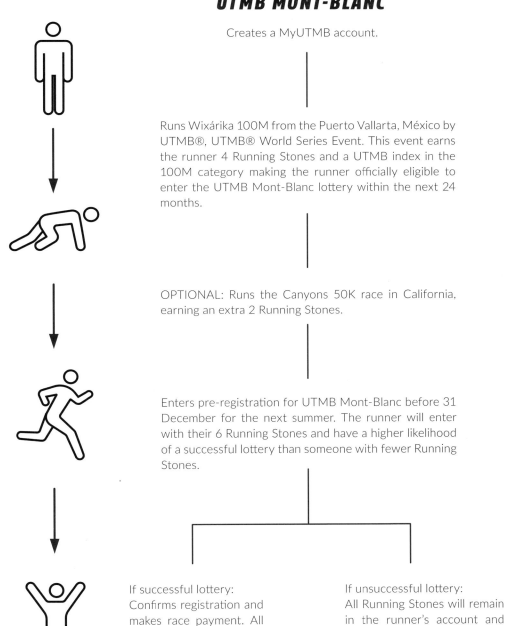

Creates a MyUTMB account.

Runs Wixárika 100M from the Puerto Vallarta, México by UTMB®, UTMB® World Series Event. This event earns the runner 4 Running Stones and a UTMB index in the 100M category making the runner officially eligible to enter the UTMB Mont-Blanc lottery within the next 24 months.

OPTIONAL: Runs the Canyons 50K race in California, earning an extra 2 Running Stones.

Enters pre-registration for UTMB Mont-Blanc before 31 December for the next summer. The runner will enter with their 6 Running Stones and have a higher likelihood of a successful lottery than someone with fewer Running Stones.

If successful lottery: Confirms registration and makes race payment. All Running Stones will be "spent."

If unsuccessful lottery: All Running Stones will remain in the runner's account and they will be able to enter with the same Running Stones and try again the following year.

But Gaylord wasn't done. At this point, he had moved on to the sports brand Columbia, where he made introductions that resulted in a seven-year partnership. And his fingerprints are even on UTMB's current partnership with the running-shoe company Hoka. Over Christmas, 2003, Gaylord met Mermoud in Snowbird, Utah, through a mutual friend. Gaylord gushed about UTMB, and the following year Mermoud ran the race. A former adventure racer, Mermoud had never run a trail race. Injured a month earlier in Chamonix, he was battling tendonitis and was forced to stop in Courmayeur, despite being in fourth place. Gaylord was right behind. Gaylord remembers seeing Mermoud in Courmayeur, where he told him, "This is crazy! I love it. I want to come back!" It was the start of a long relationship between Mermoud and UTMB.

The HOKA partnership, a three-year deal that goes well into seven figures a year, was another big leap forward. UTMB had been in talks with several possible marquee race sponsors and had received three good offers. The UTMB-HOKA partnership made the most sense, however, as Hoka was already a partner with Ironman.

AN HONOR TO RUN WITH YOU

Fourteen years after his first appearance at UTMB, Kilian Jornet returned to the start line at Place du Triangle de l'Amitié, under the tricolor in front of the mayor's office. So much had changed. Jornet was now the guy to beat, and no one ever beat him unless he was having an off day.

Which, at this occasion, might have been the case. A few weeks earlier, Jornet had tested positive for COVID, and although he was now testing negative, training had been hard. "I wasn't feeling normal. I was sweating a lot. I could train slowly, but when I reached a high pulse, I had pain in my chest and legs. I thought, okay, I can't go fast. It might be dangerous."

Despite COVID, Jornet was having a great summer. UTMB would be his third 100-mile race of the year, and at Sierre-Zinal he had turned in his second-fastest time in 12 starts.

He decided to race, wearing a mask at the start to protect his fellow runners. Once again, he was oddly in sync with the event, which was in a sense also battling COVID. This was his 500th time at a start line for a trail-running or ski-touring race, and his 6th go at UTMB. 2008's novice twenty-year-old mountain runner had become the sage of the field with three wins under his belt. At the start, he was relaxed. "I knew I was in good shape, and that I could manage the 100-mile distance well. I tried to concentrate, to not go out too fast, to not make a big thing of it."

In the intervening years, Jornet's outlook on his races had become more centered. "When I was young, races were everything. Now, I realize it's just a race. Things will happen out there and there is nothing you can do about it, so why stress about it?"

UTMB, meanwhile, was now a major international brand, powered by a partnership with one of the world's largest sports-marketing companies, with commercial partners paying six and seven figures to be listed

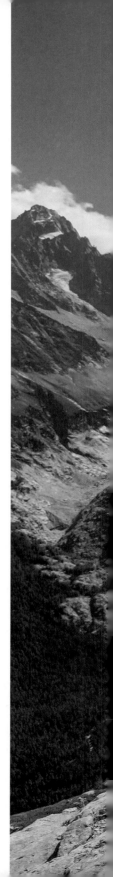

as sponsors. What had been two races when Jornet first participated had become nine events, including two competitions for children. Ten thousand runners and another twenty thousand friends and supporters packed downtown Chamonix during the last week of August, quadrupling the population, according to UTMB survey data. And if anyone wondered about the global significance of the race, the Sommet Mondial du Trail tagline ("World Summit of Trail-Running") on the fluttering street banners throughout Chamonix left no doubt about who was leading the way.

If UTMB was bringing in money, it was also costing plenty to produce, too—annually, about three million euros for the entire week of events, according to Catherine Poletti. One hundred thousand euros go to professional safety staff across the three countries. As for their own salaries, Michel Poletti puts it this way: "We have always just paid ourselves as middle managers, not as CEOs." Each year, he said, UTMB tries to save fifty thousand euros to invest in developing the event.

Chamonix itself had changed, too. The mountain town rooted in alpinism was now largely a trail-running town in the summer. By one count, nearly two dozen trail races started or ended in Chamonix each year. Elites from around the world were moving to the area to live and train. Chamonix was, simply, crazy for trail running.

Just nine months before the race, Jornet had also left his longtime brand partner, Salomon, and was deep into launching his own brand, NNormal. At the race, he was clad head to toe in new gear, with a NNormal cap, tank top, race shorts, SL race vest, and the new NNormal Kjerag shoes. A few hundred meters away, at the Ultra-Trail Village, staff at the NNormal booth were swamped with interest. After the race, Jornet told trail-running journalist Bryon Powell of *iRunFar*, "I think we need to use less gear, and we need to make gear that lasts longer... I'm super happy and I'm almost more proud of that than the results of the races."

So much had changed since 2008. But one thing had remained the same: there was still the epic 100-mile UTMB course ahead, through the corners of three countries and around Mont Blanc, and someone was going to run it faster than everyone else.

At UTMB 2022, the men's race came down to a dramatic finish between Jornet and the French runner Mathieu Blanchard.

Halfway into the race, things got interesting. "Jim [Walmsley] started to attack on the downhill into Arnouva," Jornet told me afterward. "I was like, okay, should I follow him?" But from the outset, Jornet was not feeling good on the downhills—remarkably, since he is consistently one of the best downhill runners in the world. And it was getting worse. "I wasn't coordinated well; I was like, 'What's going on here?' It was very weird. Mentally, I was out of the race." Walmsley took off.

Shortly after, as the race moved into Switzerland at the 100-kilometer mark, Matheiu Blanchard found himself just behind Jornet. And just before the climb up to Champex-Lac, Blanchard caught up to Jornet. "He said, 'Oh, Kilian, I'm sorry to pass you.' I told him, 'You are racing great, go for your race. Jim is slowing down. You'll catch him!'" Jornet tried to forget about everything and just stay close to Blanchard.

Blanchard later told the epic story on Dylan Bowman's *Freetrail* podcast. He explained that moments before he caught Jornet, he had heard that the Catalan runner planned to drop out of the race. "I realized I had two choices," he told Bowman, "to run past and [try to] give him a knockout blow, or to stop at the aid station at Champex-Lac and motivate him." Blanchard chose the latter. "I'd rather finish second [with Kilian in the race] than win [without him]. And I would do it all over again if I had the choice."

Together, the two ran on and passed a heavily fatigued Walmsley in the next leg of the race. "Jim had exploded," Jornet said.

"Now what do we do?" Blanchard asked Jornet.

"Now the race begins," Jornet answered—136 kilometers into UTMB.

After Champex-Lac, Jornet realized he had a unique challenge on his hands. "If I am racing Jim [Walmsley] or François [D'Haene], I know them as runners. But I didn't know Mathieu in this way." Jornet put his years of racing experience and strategic thinking to work. Three big climbs remained. "On the first uphill, I studied him. I pushed to see if he could follow. I wanted to know, is he a pusher or more of a steady runner? I knew I was not doing well on the downhills, so I wanted to find out how much time he could recover on the downhills. From Champex to Trient, my goal was to understand him as a runner." Back and forth, they hammered each other hard, Jornet with the advantage on the climbs, Blanchard passing on the downhills that Jornet was finding so hard.

Then came Vallorcine, 153 kilometers into the race. The scene was dramatic as the two came into the aid station together. "It was like *The Good, the Bad and the Ugly*," Blanchard said, referencing the epic final duel in the Clint Eastwood film. "We were staring each other in the eyes. We stopped for maybe thirty seconds." Leaving the aid station, Kilian took off fast. "I thought he was crazy. I thought he was going to explode," Blanchard recalled on *Freetrail*.

But from studying Blanchard since Champex-Lac, Jornet knew exactly what he needed to do. "I knew he would gain 5 minutes on the final downhill, so I knew I had to make my move after Vallorcine." Jornet took the lead by 4 minutes after just 4 kilometers. "I knew I could sustain this pace for some time, and it worked."

That is not to say it was easy for Jornet. When he arrived in Chamonix, both the race and COVID had taken its toll. Jornet looked exhausted. "I was super, super tired," he said. Still, he reveled in the battle with Blanchard. "It was not like managing the gaps," he told me, referencing so many races before where he had been out front. "It was so fun to race with him and have a real competition." Personalities matter to Jornet, too. "Mathieu is a really nice guy. He raced at a super, super high level. It was fun to race with him. The race felt like a master class."

"The most fun thing about the race was that I was running 100 miles like I run a short distance," Jornet said. "It's more than just setting your pace and go and go and go. It was strategic. It's, 'here I want to save some energy, here I want to attack.'"

The two made trail-running history, both completing the full UTMB course in under twenty hours. It was a goal never before achieved despite the efforts of nearly all of the world's best long-distance trail runners. Jornet, however, saw it coming. "Under 20 hours, I was sure it was going to happen. With all of the competition and the good weather conditions, I was thinking, 'If you want to win, you're going to have to go under 20.'"

Jornet crossed the line in 19:49:30; Blanchard finished 5 minutes and 20 seconds later and collapsed. A photo at the finish shows Blanchard on the ground, smiling up at his hero, Jornet, down at his side. "Mat, it was an honor to run with you," a re-masked Jornet said. "This time of under 20 hours, it's thanks to you. It was one of the best races of my life." Mathieu Blanchard, who had started running ultra-trail races in 2017 and joined Salomon's international team in 2022 , had been inspired in part by Kilian's autobiography and his many films.

Amid all the money, amid all the business, the egos, the brands, the hype, and the wrangling for global dominance, two of the world's greatest trail runners reminded anyone paying even casual attention that all that really mattered was the trail, the effort, and the sportsmanship. This finish will go down as one of the greatest moments in the history of the sport.

"We transcended ourselves," said Blanchard. Months later, a Photo-shopped version of the image of Jornet and Blanchard appeared, featuring the two runners on a tropical beach with palm trees. It became an Internet meme. Jornet shared it with his 1.4 million Instagram followers.

Jornet, for his part, was still very much the same wonderful soul he was in 2008—passionate for the mountains, quietly charting his own course and doing his own thing. "The mountains are really what makes him tick," said Hillary Gerardi, a professional American trail runner based in Chamonix, who has stood atop podiums with Jornet and shares his deep concern for taking care of the alpine ecosystem in which they both play so hard. "He has this really strong feeling that he wants to take care of it. He's reached a place in his career and his understanding of the environ-mental crisis and climate change [where] he knows it's time to give back." Jornet has recently launched the Kilian Jornet Foundation, which finances projects aimed at solving environmental problems in the mountains.

In the fourteen years since his first start, Jornet has won the UTMB four times and set—and reset—the course record. On the surface, much had changed for Kilian, for Chamonix, and for UTMB. But away from the dramatic spotlight of the finish line, was trail running's soul still intact at UTMB? For Michel Poletti, the balancing of business and values feels like climbing one of the dozens of serrated aretes that slice through the Chamonix skyline.

"Can we do good business and keep trail running's values?" Michel once asked me, rhetorically. "I imagine a virtual world with a ridge. On the left you have the values, on the right you have the 'bad' things—but they are not only bad. It's about making profit to invest and develop the company. It's a very narrow ridge, like PTL," Poletti said, referencing the sometimes terrifyingly airy moments during UTMB's most technical event.

It's an apt metaphor. Step too far toward business and you plummet into the abyss of profit-making. The other way lies an unsustainable com-pany. Balance perfectly, and you can move forward, the summit in sight.

Unlike climbers moving through a pristine mountain scene, however, UTMB was being watched by hundreds of thousands of passionate runners—some of whom thought it was not doing any balancing at all.

JIM WALMSLEY: "I SEE UTMB AS A CATALYST"

No elite trail runner in recent years has committed more of himself to UTMB than Jim Walmsley in his quest to win. After three attempts, the US ultrarunner from Flagstaff, Arizona, moved to France in spring, 2022, with his wife, Jesse Brazeau. The two now live in an old chalet in the quiet village of Arêches, in the Beaufortain region. They are within sight of Mont Blanc, but away from the bustle of Chamonix. In his fourth effort at UTMB, Walmsley landed in fourth place. (See page 28) Living in the Alps, up the street from four-time UTMB winner François D'Haene, Walmsley hopes to deepen his knowledge of Alps trail running.

For me, the UTMB fire was lit in 2016 after I started being pretty competitive in the U.S. trail and ultra scene. Although, ironically, I had actually been at UTMB back in 2012, when I was in Europe for a track race. At the time, I thought it sounded like the dumbest thing I had ever heard of—I wasn't into ultras yet—but I think I still kept the flier they were passing out.

When I first lined up for UTMB, it was only my third hundred mile race and my first time running with a headlamp, backpack, and poles. I was the fittest guy on the line, but that doesn't get you very far. There are different challenges at UTMB. At home, with Western States for example, I've solved that problem, I've learned how to "beat that course."

But at UTMB, I've lost by over an hour to others. So, other people have still figured it out better. I'm kind of addicted to trying over and over again to solve a problem. And I've also realized that the European mindset around training, mountains, and ultra is very different. That keeps drawing me back to UTMB.

I appreciate how European ultra runners are trying to solve the ultra problem from a different approach. For example, François D'Haene, who I really respect, his biggest effort before Hardrock was a 24-hour push on the bike. And that's not uncommon for the European elite.

In 2022, my wife Jess and I moved to France before the race. With all the challenges of moving, it didn't feel like an advantage. It was more like I was an American who came over early, rather than having time to really embrace the European thought process. Winter in the Alps is different, though. No winter running, just skis, so I've had to actually change how I train. I still don't know if it will work for me, or if moving to Europe will turn out to be just a dumb idea.

Either way, I see UTMB as a catalyst. It's a goal I'm using to help push myself as an athlete and as a person. It's a centerpiece that I am fixated on for now. I kind of jokingly say I'm not a good ultra runner because it generally takes me a few tries, but I am stubborn and I stick with my goals. And I think whatever problems I end up solving with the UTMB course will apply to the toughest mountain ultras in the world.

RORY BOSIO: "A STORYBOOK APPEAL"

Rory Bosio prefers to stay out of the limelight and no longer runs competitively, but her 2013 UTMB win, 7th place overall, will keep her forever in the race's highlight reels. Elite ultrarunner David Laney views this run as one of the greatest ultra trail runs, ever. "I always go back to that effort. Everyone should look at her splits. It was the most perfect ultra ever run." Her women's course record, 22:37:26, stood for eight years—and she followed it up with a subsequent win in 2014.

I can still see the picture that hooked me: a photo of Krissy Moehl in *Trail Runner* magazine from her 2009 UTMB win. She's going up some switchbacks with poles and there was also another picture of her coming into the finish line in Chamonix. From then on, UTMB held a storybook appeal for me. You get to go race in this beautiful, magical place where people love trails and running. The mountains are so extreme and, to me, more beautiful than what we have in the U.S.

All my role models from that time made UTMB seem like the coolest, most challenging thing ever. Lizzy Hawker, who was a main driver of my getting into trail running, had won UTMB so many times. I thought, "I have to go run that race that Lizzy's done. It's the most challenging race out there and if that's her jam, then I want to do it, too."

But I was super intimidated by the course. I really just wanted to complete the race. That would have been enough. So, honestly, I was truly surprised at how well I did. At one point, when I was told I was in first place, I asked, "Are you sure? There must be a woman in front of me. I shouldn't be in first."

Looking back, it's true that the course is well suited to me. I'm not speedy or fast. UTMB has these long, grinding climbs followed by long downhills and you just repeat that pattern nine times. That worked well for me. But, I was still definitely surprised by my 2013 win and a little overwhelmed with

the massive response I received, and how it changed my running career—starting right at the finish.

Many people have asked me what happened as I crossed the line, tried to sit down, and Catherine Poletti pulled me back up. I had just run probably my best race ever, I was super tired, and all I wanted to do was rest—but it wasn't enough. I still needed to perform and dance for the crowd at the finish.

It would be easy to look at the video of the incident and say, "Wow, Catherine is kind of heartless." But honestly, I wasn't mad. I thought it was kind of hilarious. Catherine wanted to create the drama of a victorious champion returning home, the spectacle of a superhero athlete. And I just wanted to sit down. It's really how she aims to shape and brand all of UTMB.

But there is no bad blood. In fact, we are very friendly and have stayed in good touch over the years. I offered vocal feedback on their women's podium depth, including refusing to return until the podium expanded. They have addressed this now and I really do appreciate how Catherine listens and makes changes.

UTMB is very different now from those early years and I both love and hate the changes. While I wouldn't run the race anymore, I would go spectate and enjoy it. The race has a storied history and I love being a part of it.

KEITH BYRNE: "IF YOU'VE GOT A COOL JOB FOR ME, I'LL COME BACK"

Originally from the UK and now living in Denver, Colorado, Keith Byrne has worked at The North Face since 1999 and attended every UTMB event since 2004. Byrne has seen UTMB grow over the years, and now is one of the key English language commentators for UTMB's Live coverage. In 2022, UTMB's Live coverage had nearly 14 million views. In total, people around the world watched more than 100 million minutes of UTMB videos.

Between 2003 and 2014, when The North Face partnered with UTMB, I was the manager for the partnership. So, 12 months of the year, my job was all things UTMB from the color of the runners' T-shirts and finisher vests to pushing for a truly international race experience. I saw the race grow exponentially.

I used to joke that my job was to make Catherine Poletti happy. I was like, "Michel, have you got any tips?" And he was like, "Good luck."

There was a clear vision that they wanted to grow this event, which we loved. Catherine and Michel, they knew the region, they knew how to build loyalty amongst the three countries and the many municipalities. Our goal was to use our marketing skills as well as our global pull and awareness to make UTMB globally renowned.

In 2014, the partnership ended between The North Face and UTMB. The North Face shifted and became committed to growing outdoor communities across the key cities in Europe. I was devastated, as I love the event. But at the same time, I said to Catherine and Michel, "Hey, this is the end of the collaboration between The North Face and UTMB but if you've got a cool job, I'll come back next year as a volunteer." And 2015 was the first year of UTMB TV.

UTMB TV became the catalyst for the next wave of growth. In year one, UTMB TV was nothing more than fixed cameras in aid stations. So as a commentator, it was great— once the top runners had gone through, you could go off for three hours and have fun. Now with the helicopters, the drones, and electric bikes, when the director says, "Two minute ad break," it's coffee... bathroom... croissant... and, "Welcome back to UTMB Live."

UTMB can be a tough place for the athletes with the huge crowds and media commitments. They know it comes with the territory. But the good news is that they will eventually be allowed to race and be on the start line with everyone else. That's one of the beauties of the sport—that you can toe the line with all your heroes.

In terms of change, I think UTMB has become the benchmark for the constant evolution of trail running. The biggest opportunity for UTMB is to help diversify trail running and break down some of the barriers that exist to access trail running in all communities. When you talk about Catherine, Michel and UTMB, this can polarize opinions within the trail running community. But I think people should also recognize how important Catherine and Michel have been to trail running. Their legacy, other than the UTMB races themselves, will be about how many people have discovered the power of trail running since 2003.

LIZZY HAWKER: "IT WAS ALL A BIT OF A SURPRISE"

Known for her gentle demeanor, yet incredible toughness in rugged terrain, no one else has more UTMB wins than Lizzy Hawker—an unmatched five times (2005, 2008, 2010, 2011, 2012). Lizzy now splits her time between Nepal and Switzerland, and while she no longer competes, she remains passionate about mountain explorations and personal discovery.

At first, I think it was just the idea of running in the Alps that caught my attention. I loved the mountains, but I'd not really done anything like a trail race in the Alps. I was finishing my PhD in the UK, and had seen an article about UTMB in a running magazine. Before that moment, I didn't even know UTMB existed. I thought I could go for a couple weeks' adventure—do some climbing and then aim to do the race at the end.

At registration, I realized I was the antithesis of the scene there. I was a bit overcome by all these tiny, fit people, dressed in the latest gear and looking like they knew what they were doing. Then there was me, dressed in holey Helly Hansen, with a borrowed rucksack, trail shoes I'd just bought, and my big mountain jacket. I felt daunted and wondered, "Why am I even entering this race?"

But we got started, had a beautiful sunset, and soon I just got into the feeling of the mountains. I loved it, especially running at night. I remember as I came into Courmayeur, the volunteers wanted to show me where the food and physios were, but I just wanted to get back out there. I was having a great time. As I left they said, "Oh, and you're the second lady!"

I couldn't quite grasp that. I didn't understand what had happened to all the other women during the night. A while later, I caught the first "lady," who was running with her husband. He saw the British flag on my bib and asked me how I could run so well in the mountains being from the UK. I thought it would be cool to be the first woman to the Swiss border, but I was sure they'd catch me there because I really didn't know what I was doing. But they didn't, and I thought, "What do I do now?" I just took it checkpoint to checkpoint, all the way to the finish. It was all a bit of a surprise.

One of the best moments was climbing up to Bovine, nearing the end. There was thick fog all around and I was totally alone. I could hear strains of music and finally, as I got closer, I saw a man sitting on the hillside playing the French horn. That's always stuck with me. It was such a beautiful moment.

Coming into Chamonix, I had never seen anything like that finish line. There were so many people. But as soon as I crossed the line, my one preoccupation was, "How am I going to get back to my tent site?" It was up in Argentière, 10 km away. I hadn't calculated finishing in the night, when the buses were no longer running. It was all so unexpected. My mom even phoned the tourist office in Chamonix the next morning to confirm I was okay, because she couldn't quite believe I had gotten back that fast.

But I did make it back and I loved it. The whole time I had in my mind a quote from *Alice In Wonderland*: "Begin at the beginning... and go on until you come to the end: then stop."

Among the 2,539 runners who started UTMB in 2006 was an unassuming 57-year-old quarry worker from the small town of Robilante in the Piedmont region of Italy. He had no coach and no sponsor. Until a year before, he had never trained on the UTMB course. But he liked to run long distances. "I'm like a donkey, not a horse," he said. His name was Marco Olmo.

Olmo liked to race. At UTMB 2006, he started out slowly. "I didn't start with the front group," he told me through an interpreter. "Instead, I ran quietly at my own pace." After sunset, the evening turned into a beautiful starry night. Olmo remembers seeing a shooting star as he crossed into his native Italy at Col de la Seigne. He wanted to make a wish on the star, but he skipped it. "Everybody saw it," he explained. "So, the wish wouldn't have counted." It turned out Olmo didn't need the star's help.

IT DIDN'T FEEL REAL

Even today, the UTMB course offers quiet moments like the one experienced by Olmo at Col de la Seigne, particularly during the night. For the runners, these moments can be very affecting. UTMB offers the opposite, as well. The finish, so very different from quiet moments on the trail, is choreographed trail-running pageantry.

For Katie Schide, winning UTMB was different from winning any other race. "It didn't feel real," she told me. "I looked at a video later and realized, 'Oh, that's me!' Once I was done, it was like... what do I do now?" Schide couldn't locate her friends among the masses behind the barriers. "It was cool to give high fives to strangers, but I really wanted to see the people who were part of it for me."

For winners of UTMB, the experience doesn't end at the finish line. "If you win UTMB, you'll not only cement your place among the pantheon of ultra-trail running's all-time greats. You'll also very likely punch your sponsorship ticket for the rest of your competitive career," said Brian Metzler, a US-based running journalist who has reported on UTMB races since 2009. "Like those who win Ironman and the Boston Marathon, you become a household name and elevate your sponsor profile forever after. And that's going to be especially true going forward, as UTMB becomes even more prominent and more competitive." For Schide, that surreal feeling is likely to continue for some time.

EVERY MOMENT, CHOREOGRAPHED

Runners like Schide are not the only ones treated to an exuberant welcome back to Chamonix. The experience extends to all the other runners as well, no matter how fast—or slow—they go. Fans join in the celebratory atmosphere, no matter the hour. UTMB organizers would say they choreograph every moment of the race not because it attracts sponsors—well, not only—but because it is amazing and inspiring that anyone could do what these runners have dared to attempt.

Nick Yardley, fifty-eight, is one of the runners UTMB has not forgotten about. He started UTMB in 2010, 2011, and 2012, finishing twice and once dropping out after 102 kilometers at Grand Col Ferret on the Swiss–Italian border. Yardley grew up in Yorkshire, England, but has lived in the United States for nearly four decades. A climbing guide early in his professional career, Yardley came to know Chamonix in his teens and twenties while tackling technical routes on the many peaks of the Mont Blanc massif.

The UTMB race experience begins well before the start, since UTMB has an unusual evening start time. While most ultra-distance races start in the early morning, UTMB sends runners off at 6:00 p.m. "You have a full day awake to contemplate what is about to happen," said Yardley. " Most races, you roll out of bed and rush to the start line." This time allows the enormity of the looming task to sink in as the day progresses.

As runners filter through town towards the starting line, a carefully organized experience begins. "They're so good at making everyone in the crowd feel special," said Yardley. "It's all about you, the community, and what you're about to experience." Added to that mix is UTMB's de facto soundtrack, Vangelis' "Conquest of Paradise." It's hard not to shed a tear or two. Yardley has experienced this, too. "I'm not a guy who cries or tears up much," he said. "But every time I've started that frigging race, I get tears in my eyes." The buildup affects the normally reserved Yardley. "It drives me nuts," he half joked. "By the time you start, you're really running on excitement and fumes. There's a lot of positive energy." He paused, then added, "You're heading off into a journey of the unknown."

Once over the start line, running down Rue du Dr. Paccard adds a different layer of intensity. "There are runners and fans just inches from your shoulder, yelling and cheering," Yardley said. "You just don't get that in any other race that I know of. It's very special."

UTMB has been a pioneer for trail running in one other regard, allowing friends and family around the world to engage with each runner. It's easy to follow runners online as they pass through key points around the course. "That makes it easy to get wrapped up in the race," said Yardley. "People globally can share in this special experience."

In 2022, Yardley experienced a paternal mix of joy and angst, watching both online and in person as his son Ben ran UTMB. "After he finished the race," he said, "Ben was blown away by how many people had followed him at every aid station."

Runners get further inspired by the knowledge that loved ones are cheering them on at home. Ben completed the loop in a very speedy 33:27:42, finishing 319th out of the 2,627 starters. "Everybody could see Ben finish, running up to the finish line and raising his hands," Nick said.

Arriving back in Chamonix is a lifetime highlight for every runner. Champagne corks are popping throughout the twenty-six hours during which the racers finish. "Even in the dead of night, there are people in the streets watching, partying, and cheering," said Yardley. "No matter what time you finish the race, there's a commentator on the microphone announcing who is finishing. They do that for hours and hours," Yardley

points out. "Every single person feels special. At a lot of races, there's big congratulations for the first twenty, and for anyone after, there's nothing." Yardley should know. He's raced dozens of ultras over the years, including other big-name events. UTMB, said Yardley, "makes the race about finishing."

None of this is by accident. From the outset, the Polettis have had the mid-pack runners in mind. "We need to never forget," said Catherine Poletti, "that the biggest part of our runners are the regular runners. Some of them fight the time cut-offs. Most of them just want to finish back in Chamonix."

Even the last runner is feted. From the early days of the race, UTMB celebrated the last finisher to come in under the 46.5 hour time limit. The runner became known as the Lanterne Rouge, a nod to the red lantern on the caboose of old-school trains. Unlike the top runners, the final finishers of UTMB have run through two nights on the course. They arrive in Chamonix to roaring crowds, often looking more than a bit dazed. UTMB's awards ceremony is choreographed to include the arrival of the Lanterne Rouge. Top racers and volunteers form a corridor in front of the finish line, while other volunteers part the sea of onlookers waiting for the awards ceremony at the world's most important trail race. The Lanterne Rouge takes the stage alongside trail-running luminaries. It's a touching visual reminder of the scope and breadth of the trail-running community.

VALUES FROM THE OUTSET

Other values that the Polettis see as core to UTMB have been highlighted by the race since the first edition. That year, UTMB distributed a small leaflet—its first print publication—on a folded sheet of paper that highlighted "Respecting the ethics of the trail: discover, but with respect to the environment and others." A year later, a much larger runner's guide talked about respecting the values of trail running.

Why the focus on values? "We had been impressed by this new sport," said Michel Poletti. "There was a new spirit in the sport that we immediately wanted to share, promote, and protect. It was a family built around camaraderie."

But while the Polettis wanted to chart their own path and imbue the race with their sense of trail running's values, in those early days there had been one huge obstacle in the way.

In 2003, they had operated the race under the auspices of the Club des Sports. And after the first edition, the Club had seen what was possible, and wasn't particularly interested in letting go.

The president wrote Bachelard a letter, offering to keep them on as volunteers in a new entity. Bachelard, along with the Polettis and Jean-Claude Marmier, refused. After all, they, had labored for a year to see the event come to fruition. They were not about to become volunteers for eternity within the Club des Sports. They had higher ambitions.

Chamonix's mayor, Michel Charlet, intervened. Club des Sports operated under the direction of the town of Chamonix, so he had the final word. In the fall of 2003, he called a meeting at the top floor of the Hotel Morgane, just a stone's throw from where the Polettis once owned their Violni record shop.

It was a testy, dramatic affair. "Beaucoup de tension," said Michel Poletti, switching to French to make certain to accurately capture the energy in the room.

Former mayor Charlet, now seventy-eight, remembers the moment. "The Polettis came to me and told me, 'This isn't working. We need to be independent.' And I understood. The town had been through something like this before with another sports event. The Club des Sports functions with public funding, so there are barriers of different kinds."

At the end of the meeting, Charlet announced his decision. The Polettis' proposal for a new organization that was one part for-profit and one part nonprofit was a good one. "The president of Club des Sports was not happy," said Michel Poletti. "They could not believe what was happening," said Catherine.

There was blowback. "The president of Club des Sports was pretty mad with me," Charlet recalls. But in Charlet's mind, it was the right thing to do. "When you're talking about a budget the size of UTMB's, there is a financial risk for Club des Sports."

In essence, the mayor of Chamonix had given UTMB to the Polettis—for nothing. After all, they had done the hard work to make the first edition a huge success, and they had a vision for the future, one that would clearly also benefit Chamonix.

The door to the future had been opened, and within months, the Polettis had created a nonprofit organization, Les Trailers du Mont-Blanc, in tandem with a new professional group, Autour du Mont Blanc—a not uncommon strategy in Europe. The directors of each body overlapped but were not identical. They were on their way up the arête, with a structure designed to balance values and business. But would it work? Could they create the sense of community they loved and grow the event?

In 2005, the first year of the new corporate structure, the nonprofit arm raised funds for Courir pour Toi, a clearing-house organization that supports nonprofits working to cure serious medical conditions. They raised 4,271 euros. Over the years, Les Trailers has expanded to fund medical research, trail work, and an environmental commission that works to improve the sustainability of the event. It now raises about 500,000 euros annually through charity race bibs, with donors giving directly to a rotating series of about twenty nonprofits. For the other work it undertakes, the organization has an annual budget of about 200,000 euros, with 14.5 euros from each UTMB race entry going towards its support.

There have been successes. The environmental commission has eliminated the use of disposable cups, organized volunteers to assure that fragile sections of the race courses are protected during the events and helped make sure that regulations are followed in the natural reserves through which UTMB races pass. The association has also funded trail work. Roadblocks with regional authorities, however, have slowed or halted some projects, most recently at a badly damaged section of the

UTMB course at Col de la Seigne. "Five years we've been talking about this work!" Michael Poletti tells me, and the frustration in his voice is unmistakable.

MISSTEPS

In the delicate management of the needs of the community and the demands of business, UTMB has made some mistakes. US elite trail runner and podcaster Dylan Bowman, who is part of the team that produces live UTMB race coverage each year, candidly observes a self-inflicted pattern, and points to the Ironman announcement as an example. "I think they're still kind of digging out from the announcement of the Ironman partnership," said Bowman. "They could have done a lot more to show the community their true ambitions and intentions, which would have preemptively tamped down some of the anger and skepticism." Bowman gives an example. "If they had come out and said, 'Here's what Ironman's bringing to the table—operating capital, event expertise—and here's the benefit to the average trail runner,' they could have helped themselves out and saved so much headache."

Ironically, one of the most contentious issues that has swirled around UTMB is that of prize money for the top runners. Ironic, because the lack of prize money stems from a noble intention enshrined in one of the earliest statements of the organization's values. The first substantial race publication, the eighteen-page "Roadbook" created for the second edition, boldly announced "Pas de Dotation en Argent" ("No Cash Prizes"). "The spirit and values of the trail come together," it explains. "Gifts for every finisher. Not for profit, only for pleasure."

PRIZE MONEY: WHOSE VALUES, ANYWAY?

"In the first years, we didn't want prize money," said Catherine Poletti. "It was a question for us of sharing the same values. We decided we'd offer the same gift to each finisher. The point of the race was for it to be fun, not for profit."

This idea didn't come out of thin air. The Polettis' previous experience of awarding cash to winners had been upsetting.

Two decades ago, Catherine Poletti served as the treasurer of the CMBM trail-running club that was part of the town's Club des Sports. CMBM managed the 23-kilometer Cross du Mont-Blanc, which was already becoming known around the world. Poletti saw Kenyan, Russian, and Ethiopian runners climb the podium and then watched helplessly as they descended directly into the arms of their coaches, who promptly presented her with invoices made out to their management companies. "I knew the money wasn't going to the athletes," she said. "It was exploitation. Honestly, it was one of the worst experiences of my life. I was shocked."

From that day on, the Polettis worried that corrupt coaches would insinuate their way into UTMB. "Maybe not with Kilian," said Catherine Poletti, "But what about the next one?"

But starting in 2012, with trail running growing rapidly, the vibe began to change. Kilian Jornet had won UTMB a second time. There were plenty of other big names developing in the sport, too, like the popular French runner Xavier Thévenard. In the first years of the race, a UTMB win bestowed fame upon an athlete. Now, though, the race benefitted from the participation of those same runners. The tables had turned.

Stung by what the Polettis had seen years earlier, UTMB resisted cash prizes. In 2018, the race surveyed elite runners to see what their preferences were. "All of them said it was now routine to have prize money," said Catherine Poletti. In the survey, the race proposed three tiers of prize money. Interestingly, the plurality of athletes chose the middle sum. "A lot of them said, 'If we go too high with prize money, the sport will not be the same,'" Catherine Poletti reported.

Finally, UTMB relented, and from 2019 to 2021, the race offered prize money ranging from 500 euros to 2,000 euros for the top ten men and top ten women. By 2022, prizes ran from 1,000 euros for finishing sixth to tenth, to 10,000 euros for finishing first. While many casual onlookers assumed Ironman was behind the change, the race's thinking was more nuanced. "We had cancelled Ultra-Trail World Tour and decided to replace it with the new World Series with the Finals at UTMB Mont-Blanc," said Michel Poletti. The prior series had prize money of up to 5000 euros for the men and women's series winners. "So," he said," for such a finals of a major international series, we thought that 10,000 euros was appropriate."

"It's a start, albeit a slow one," said Tim Tollefson (see page 82), an elite athlete based in Mammoth Lakes, California. "A UTMB victory currently remains more valuable in sponsorship leverage than race-day earnings." Tollefson is a loyal participant in UTMB. In 2016 and 2017, he finished third. "It's a huge business and yet the prize money has been laughable," he notes. Tollefson points out that other elite athletes have strong feelings, too. "One of them suggested we boycott UTMB until they start to legitimately compensate athletes," he said. "We're on the losing end of this deal."

Tollefson has had the conversation about prize money with the Polettis and Andrew Messick. "Michel brought up the importance of amateurism," Tollefson said. "I was like, 'Respectfully, that is an antiquated narrative that needs to change. Professional athletes need to make money.' And Andrew, because he comes from a different world, he backed it up."

The Polettis still worry about the corrupting influence of money, including the temptation to dope. "I don't want drug users winning our races," said Catherine Poletti bluntly.

"As revenue grows, that capital can do good for this sport," said Tollefson. "Compensate the talent while also investing in a framework of out-of-competition testing to protect the integrity of these events."

Trail running, particularly in Europe, has already had cases of top athletes doping to win, and big cash awards clearly add to the incentive for ethically challenged runners. Petro Mamu, Christel Dewalle, and Elisa Desco are all top runners who have either been reprimanded or served suspensions after being caught doping. Swiss runner Maude Mathys, who

has won high profile trail races around the world—many of them several times—was given a warning after a positive test. One of the most famous trail races in the world, Switzerland's Sierre-Zinal, experienced two high-profile cases as recently as 2022. The men's winner tested positive for two banned substances and received a four-year suspension from the sport. And the woman's winner was also suspended after a May, 2022 positive test came to light—leaving the victory, with a certain irony, to Mathys.

And UTMB is certainly not immune. In 2015, the Ecuadorian runner Gonzalo Calisto finished fifth at UTMB. His name turned up on a list of suspended runners following a post-race blood test at UTMB. He was subsequently disqualified.

In 2022, however, UTMB made another false step, giving fuel to its critics. Italy's Martina Valmassoi, a popular, savvy, and free-spirited trail runner with a big social-media following, battled hard to win the 145-kilometer TDS race on August 23, near the start of a week of UTMB races.

"On the race website, they had written that there would be prize money for UTMB, CCC, OCC, and TDS," said Valmassoi. The amounts were never stated, but Valmassoi had talked with previous winners. "Sometimes it was a thousand euros, sometimes two thousand euros." At the race's prize ceremony, Valmassoi got a trophy and a backpack, but no information was forthcoming about her cash winnings. Valmassoi asked around. Top-ten finishers in UTMB, CCC and OCC—races that are part of the new World Series events—all received money, with winners getting 10,000 euros each.

On September 6, Valmassoi emailed the race organizers. She didn't receive a reply. A week later, she wrote again, this time receiving a reply from a race official apologizing for the lack of response and saying, "Congratulations for your very impressive performance on TDS 2002. UTMB Mont-Blanc organization does not distribute Prize Money on TDS."

Valmassoi asked again but received no reply. UTMB's apparent unwillingness to offer an explanation, or even say that discussions were ongoing, convinced her to go public, which she did on September 14. Her Instagram post received nearly four hundred comments and over seven thousand likes, including far-ranging criticism of UTMB for its lack of clarity and responsiveness. A number of the comments were from elite athletes and other trail-running professionals.

"When it's written, and you don't do what you write on the rules, that's wrong," Valmassoi said. Finally, eleven days after the post, UTMB wrote her again, saying in part, "Congratulations on your first place on TDS 2022… we are delighted to inform you that… you will receive the amount of 1,300 euros." It wasn't the 10,000 euros of UTMB's three big World Series finals, but that had never been promised.

UTMB had erred. Despite finally correcting its mistake and apologizing on social media, the damage was done. And Valmassoi? She remains rightfully nonplussed. "They fucked up," she said. "You can fuck up, but when someone points at it, you should do better."

When I asked her about it, Catherine Poletti agreed the race had messed up. "This year, we made a mistake, to be honest, a real mistake." She explained how it had come about. "Simply, we forgot. When I saw Martina's message, I said [to my staff], 'She's right.' The organization didn't have enough money to pay her the same amount as the other races, but we looked for a way to somehow recognize her."

How could a race organization simply forget about prize money? Poletti explained that TDS was an outlier. Since it was not part of the new UTMB World Series, the organization had tried to move it to a separate date. That proved impossible, so the TDS race was held during the UTMB week. But the race organization still wanted it to be something different, a race for runners who wouldn't have to go through the new World Series qualifying process. In all of the shifting change for TDS, the organization had somehow neglected revisiting the issue of prizes.

"WTF? WHERE ARE THE OTHER WOMEN?"

A decade before Valmassoi had to push the organization to acknowledge they owed her prize money, UTMB course record setter Rory Bosio had already pointed out a serious inequity. The year was 2012, and Bosio had placed fourth in UTMB. It was her first European trail race.

"On the podium, they called up ten men, but only five women," said Bosio. "I was like, 'What the fuck?' "

Bosio returned the following year, won the women's race, and came in seventh overall, setting a women's course record in the process. Still, there were only five women on the podium. UTMB at the time was part of a European podium norm that too often had fewer women than men. The twisted logic said that so few women raced, the tenth-place female finisher—often with a resulting time that was mid-pack— was not worthy of accolades. "I found the race plenty competitive!" she said. After the race, Catherine Poletti emailed her congratulations and expressed surprise that Bosio was unhappy with the gender mismatch on the podium.

By 2014, Bosio was really getting frustrated. "I came back to race again, and this time, I was just pissed." After the race—which she won again—she brought up the topic over dinner with Catherine Poletti. "It was the same thing," Bosio said. "That the women's field was not competitive enough to call up ten runners. I found it so surprising and super frustrating."

When she was invited back the following year, Bosio declined. She wrote back and explained why. Finally, in 2016, the women's podium was expanded to ten, matching the number of men receiving recognition and awarding them equal prize money.

"Sometimes, they need a swift kick in the butt to change," said Bosio, touching upon a theme of reactivity that runs through UTMB's missteps over the years. "That's unfortunate."

"I'm a card-carrying feminist," Bosio adds. "It just really got under my skin. It bothered me because I held so much reverence for the race, and we were being told, 'You women just aren't quite there.'"

Through it all, Bosio appreciated Catherine Poletti's demeanor. "Cath-

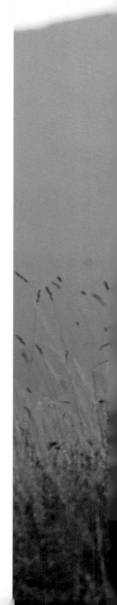

WOMEN IN UTMB

TIME GAP BETWEEN FIRST MAN AND FIRST WOMAN

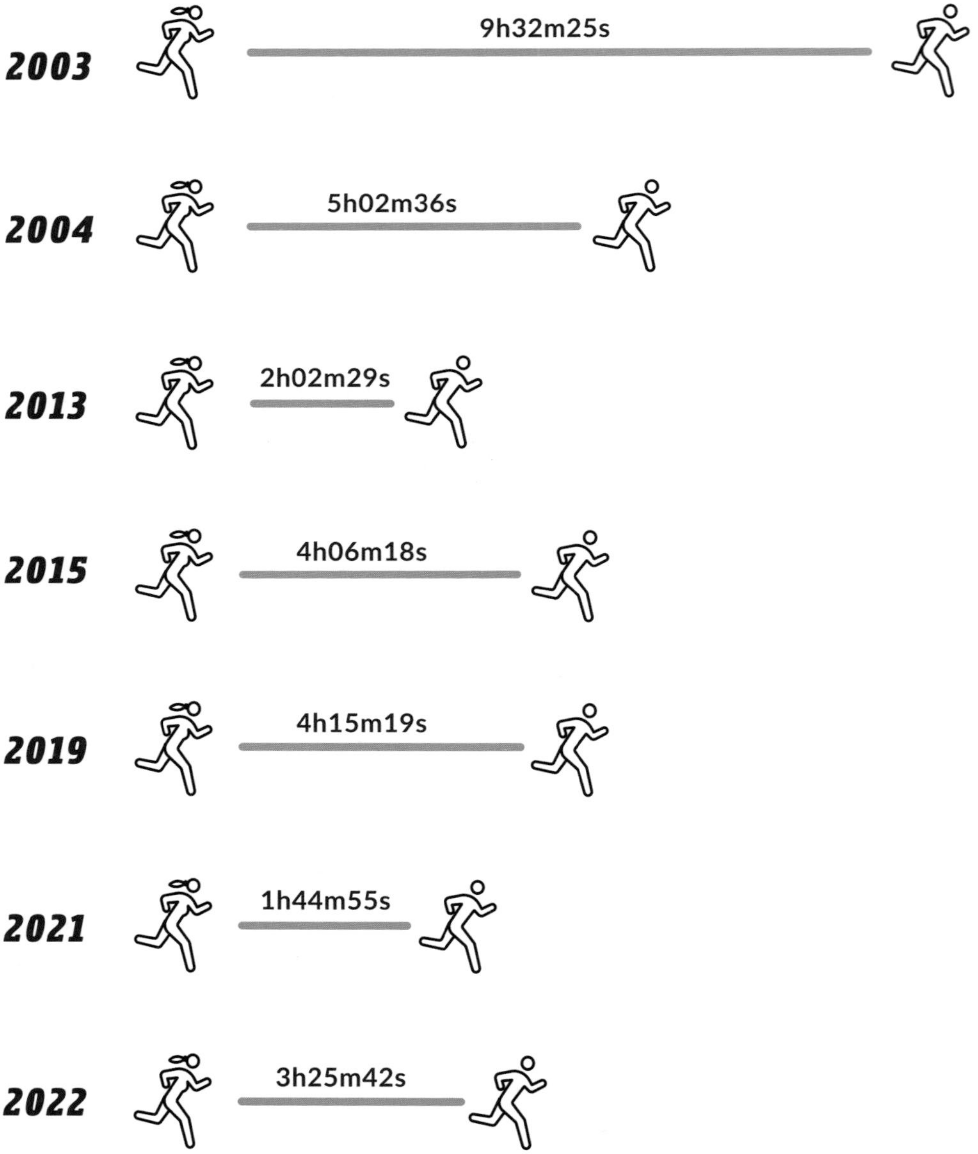

2003 — 9h32m25s

2004 — 5h02m36s

2013 — 2h02m29s

2015 — 4h06m18s

2019 — 4h15m19s

2021 — 1h44m55s

2022 — 3h25m42s

WOMEN IN UTMB OVER THE YEARS

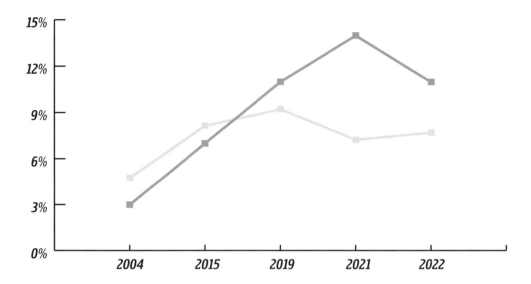

- % of women in the top 100
- % of women finishers

erine and I are very friendly. There was never any bad blood between us. It was always like, 'This is something we can talk about as adults.'"

"When you make a decision, you have only your own opinion and the opinions of the people around you," said Catherine Poletti. "Sometimes it takes someone like Rory to come with constructive criticism."

It was an interesting explanation, because it unintentionally pointed out a quirk of the organization about which observers continue to comment—that UTMB race managers were and are still too insular, and too often the result has been decision-making that was tone-deaf. In other words, too many unforced errors.

Layered over all of it, too, was a complex cultural filter. UTMB, a race grounded deeply in the French trail running world, was now very much an international race. And when it came to gender discussions, it seemed as though on some days there was a chasm between cultures. The US, for example, often leads international discussion, even if the country's politics are more complicated. So, for example, it makes a certain amount of sense that it was an American runner who raised the issue. ("It is interesting to note that our 'way of thinking' had not been seen as 'against women's rights' for more than 10 years," said Poletti, "Until we were questioned by Rory.")

In implementation of the earlier podium policy, Michel Poletti views it like this: "In some cultures, finding balance means strict equality between men and women. Ten women and ten men on the podium," he said. "In other cultures, it may not mean strict equality, but rather matching the percentage of rate of participation." Poletti, who ran the Western States Endurance Race in 2015 and again in 2018, told me their podiums had 10 women and 10 men. "We saw how this was managed in the US," he said, "and we saw they were right, and we made the change."

In 2019, Bosio ran the UTMB International race in Ushuia, Argentina, winning the women's race and coming in ninth overall. Since then, she has gradually left trail racing generally and UTMB in particular. "UTMB is a giant, and they have a quest for global dominance," she said. "And I've always appreciated the sleepy, quirky qualities of trail running."

UTMB has been lagging the global trend of trail races working to level a playing field that has been historically tilted against women. For years, the race offered deferrals to injured runners, but not to runners who become pregnant, considering pregnancy a choice that a runner made. But, as North Face athlete Stephanie Case pointed out in a 2017 article in *Outside* magazine, "Pregnancy is not simply a matter of choice... All sorts of possibilities, including accidents and surprises, come into play." A public outcry ensued, and the race changed the policy, but not until 2021.

The issue, wrote Case, "is just about recognizing women as complete human beings." Now, years later, Case has personal experience in the matter. She recently miscarried, and now hopes to get pregnant again. "Training for an ultra requires you to be all-in," Case said. "There needs to be an allowance for how much both trying to get pregnant and getting pregnant changes your life, your running plans, your training, motivation, and planning. And there's recovery, too," she adds. "Recovering from preg-

nancy takes a long time."

UTMB 2022 had a few other missteps as they worked to implement new policies. A new directive on assistance at aid stations left the world's top trail runners scrambling for help in the hours leading up to the start of the race. The change was well intentioned, the result of a new, race-inspired environmental policy that implemented two additional road closures, designed to decrease the number of cars circulating around Mont Blanc during the race. But the rollout was uneven.

Sometime during the summer, the top runners had received an email from UTMB announcing changes to access to the aid stations for their crews. "But we all get a ton of emails from UTMB," points out Katie Schide. Schide, like most other racers with whom I talked, put the email aside.

Then, the week before the race, word began circulating that there would be road closures to key access points, and the only way to get to them was via UTMB shuttle. The only problem? There were not enough seats to go around, and the few that existed had long since been snapped up.

Suddenly, the world's top trail racers would have no pit crew at key locations. Imagine racing the Indianapolis 500 and having to change the tires yourself. Elite athletes began contacting their managers, who also felt they were being left in the dark. A lot of frantic people were trying to figure out how to get to key positions in the race. One major brand planned to pre-position vehicles within the closed sections to shuttle crew back and forth.

A few days before the race, UTMB announced that vehicle passes would be made available for runners with a certain elite ranking score on the UTMB Index.

To the elite runners, it looked like another UTMB mistake. The story is often more complex, however, as it was in this case. Runners—like so many of us—skipped quickly through crowded email inboxes. In July, UTMB's bus partner announced they had fewer busses than anticipated. And the policy was designed with the mass of UTMB runners in mind, without considering the much faster pace of elite runners. The end result was a pre-race rush by all sides to find a solution. In the eleventh hour, the issue was resolved when the organization made additional vehicle passes available. The snafu was a clear example of a well-intentioned policy whose implementation was both complex and not thoroughly thought through. At UTMB, where top runners train all year for the start line and a chance to stand atop the podium has lifelong consequences, every move must be considered with care. Anything less can end up as a very public face plant. In the end, the whole affair points out the perils of decision-making without engaging with stakeholders—in this case, top brands and their runners.

Despite the reorganization of corporate governance and the addition of a multinational sports-marketing company, more changes are still needed at UTMB if future errors are to be avoided. "It's been difficult to maintain the quality in a company that has grown so much in the past two years," said Michel Poletti. "But as always, we learn from our mistakes. We'll be as perfect as we can."

And, of course, the race is not monolithic. There are internal disagreements between staff, executives, and owners, and as with any growing company, one must imagine that the best choices do not always surface. "Michel and I, we are very different. Sometimes we have strong, passionate discussions. Sometimes," Catherine said with a laugh, "we even fight. Ultimately, it gives us a stronger perspective."

Reflecting on the errors the race has made over the years, Catherine Poletti made an observation about their decision making that many wish would be more thoroughly implemented. "It's not enough," she said. "We need to listen to others."

THE ARÊTE CAN'T GO ON FOREVER

Michel Poletti's imaginary arête is a wonderful metaphor, but like all metaphors, it only goes so far. Climbers moving up an airy ridge are on their own, but unlike a climb, each bold step forward for UTMB comes with consequences for others. As Topher Gaylord pointed out to me, "UTMB doesn't dictate what trail running is, but they are an outsized directional force."

Take, for example, the sheer numbers. UTMB is an enormous economic engine for the entire Chamonix valley. It's the biggest event of the year. Before the race, the valley's summer season hit a wall come mid-August, and by the end of the month, the area had fallen headlong into the interseason between summer and winter. Now, the busy season goes right through UTMB week and to the start of September. UTMB brings with it 55,000 nights spent at hotels in Chamonix and an additional 30 percent jump in business revenue.

But it's a mixed blessing. During UTMB week, the valley feels congested. The appearance of the UTMB banners that deck lamp posts around town sometimes causes consternation in locals. Thirteen thousand people live in the valley, and there's room for another eighty-two thousand visitors. UTMB-related visitors approach that cap, something that otherwise happens only during prime vacation times: the first two weeks of August and Christmas week. Ian Dove is co-owner of Moody Coffee Roasters, a popular hangout for trail runners. The business benefits greatly from UTMB traffic, but as a valley resident, he also struggles with the impacts of that traffic. "It's a crazy time," he said. "Everything and everyone—the services, the businesses, the workers—is pushed to its limits. It's not just the athletes. We feel like we do our own ultra-marathon during that week! Despite all that, we love it. It's exhilarating and inspiring."

That congestion is particularly severe at UTMB time. "It's because everyone is in the same place at the same time—downtown to watch all the races," said Nicolas Durochat, Director of Chamonix's Office of Tourism. "In fact, there are no more tourists in Chamonix during UTMB week than there are during each of the first three weeks of August." Durochat's office uses data provided by the telecommunications company Orange,

UTMB MONT-BLANC WEEK

TIMETABLE

The timing of races during UTMB week is carefully choreographed

MONDAY	TUESDAY	WEDNESDAY	THURSDAY	FRIDAY	SATURDAY	SUNDAY
PTL MONDAY 8:00–SUNDAY 16:30						
MCC 10:00–20:15						
	TDS TUE 00:00–WED 20:00					
	YCC 11:00–15:00					
	ETC 14:00–18:00					
		YCC THE REVENGE 13:00–15:00				
			OCC 08:15–23:45			
				CCC FRI 09:00–SAT 18:00		
				UTMB FRI 18:00–SUN 16:40		

165

which tracks the total number of cell phones in the valley. The tourism office hopes to work with the mayor's office and UTMB to find ways to mitigate the impact of the crush. Durochat suggests such ideas as obligatory parking outside of downtown, race viewing stands down-valley, or even charging to see the start and finish, as many major international sporting events do.

Eric Fournier is the mayor of Chamonix. In a conversation at his office, two stories above the UTMB start line, he told me that he believes UTMB is at a turning point. Fournier acknowledged that, even as the race strengthens global awareness of Chamonix, not every local resident is enthusiastic.

"In the last few years, we've seen the race take on a new dimension. There are some concerns that are generated with the arrival of Ironman. With them, the model is not the same," he said, referencing the need for merchandise sales and big participant numbers. "The question facing us is, do we know how to make an event that is both a global event and also a local event? How can UTMB maintain a strong connection to the region? I will not pretend that we have found an answer. And it is crucial to find a response, because UTMB needs to continue to be accepted by the region."

Fournier, by the way, knows UTMB not just as a resident. In hyperactive Chamonix, it makes perfect sense that the mayor is also an avid trail runner. He's run UTMB's 100-kilometer CCC race twice, and the 56-kilometer OCC three times. (In fact, I scheduled my interview with him when we crossed paths on a remote trail, high above the Chamonix valley.) He's recently qualified for the lottery for next year's CCC, too, but will run the OCC only if his twenty-seven-year-old son runs with him. "My son runs less," he said. (Can the mayor receive a special exception to the lottery? "Catherine is totally incorruptible on this issue," he told me, laughing.)

The impacts go beyond raising the blood pressure of locals, of course, and include how the guests move about the valley, and even what sort of food UTMB provides the invading army of trail runners.

In 2017, to address those issues, the race joined nineteen other sporting events in France in partnering with the country's chapter of the World Wildlife Fund. The pact included an assessment of the race's carbon impact and called for the training of environmental ambassadors and additional sustainable development work. The sourcing of local organic food is one area where UTMB is making changes.

"When we make a big order at SuperU, we need to make sure we're buying cheese and meat that is local and organic," said Michel Polleti, referring to the national supermarket chain that has three locations in the valley. "And the percentage of local organic food increases each year."

Then there's the question of how the visitors get around in Chamonix. "It's the duty of the company to improve our transportation," said Michel Poletti, acknowledging complaints from residents. "We've pushed visitors to make use of UTMB-sponsored shuttles and buses, but we need to do more."

There are global impacts, too. UTMB entices runners from around the world in an era when international air travel is coming under scrutiny for its profound impact on climate change, and when some notable European trail runners are making pledges to reduce or eliminate their personal air travel. It's a fact not lost on the race, which is already being criticized in some quarters.

"It's particularly an issue with the UTMB World Series," Michel Poletti told me. "First, we need to reduce our impact; then we need to offset the carbon emissions." He anticipates the addition of a carbon calculator to the race registration pages and imagines a day when runners might enter a "red zone" with their carbon emissions, at which point they would be required to pay to offset the impact of their travel, or perhaps no longer receive lottery entries for the Chamonix races. It's a hopeful sign, but as of today the fundamental structure of the race series encourages maximum international travel by runners who want to increase their odds of being in one of the prestigious races at the end of each August.

To move more quickly on sustainability, the UTMB Group has hired two employees to work on environmental initiatives, moving much of the work from the nonprofit association to the professional group. "Now we need to be acting to make changes, not just talking about them," Poletti said.

But can an event like UTMB, which draws ten thousand runners from around the globe to run through fragile alpine environments, ever be considered sustainable? Can the carrying capacity of the narrow, rugged Chamonix valley really be calculated solely by the available number of hotel beds? In the years to come, UTMB and the town will have to answer these questions or face justified criticism.

But the push for sustainability may collide with the Polettis' vision. "If you don't grow, you fail," Catherine Poletti once told me.

"We want to keep this event at the top of the trail-running world," Michel added. "We worked day and night for years to develop this event. We put a lot of energy and passion into it." He then listed several events that have lost their spot at the top over the generations, including Les Templiers and Diagonale des Fous.

But the balance of business and community is still very much a work in progress, and the Polettis recognize this. "When we announced the deal with Ironman, we heard from a lot of people worried that we take care of the spirit of UTMB, and not change it into the triathlon spirit. We need to keep our authenticity and the originality of the race. We need to not be like every other major sporting event. My biggest concern is that we stay focused on the needs of trail running." Asked for an example, Michel Poletti talks about marketing. "We need to communicate like any other big sporting event, but we need to do it with our heart and soul. We are in Chamonix, not Paris."

FOOD AT MAJOR AID STATIONS

Aid stations are havens along the course where runners can get food, fluids, showers, sleep, medical assistance, and sports massages.

FLUIDS

- Plain water
- Sparkling water
- Energy drinks
- Cola
- Coffee
- Tea
- Noodle soup
- Vegetable soup

FOOD

- Cereal bars
- Sweet cakes
- Chocolate
- Dried apricots
- Dried figs
- Bananas
- Oranges
- Watermelon
- Lemon
- Salty biscuits
- Cheese
- Sausage
- Bread
- A hot dish is served at Les Chapieux, Maison Vieille, Courmayeur, Champex-Lac and at the race finish in Chamonix.

FOREVER YOUNG

Fortunately for UTMB, a seemingly endless stream of entrants re-energize the spirit of the race around Mont Blanc every August. No one exemplifies that better than the modest Marco Olmo. "When I started running on the road into Chamonix," Olmo said, "I saw lots of people. I realized they were all clapping for me. I didn't know where I was, but suddenly I didn't feel tired." On that day in August 2006, despite being one of the older runners on the course, Olmo won the UTMB, fulfilling the wish he had wanted to make hours earlier at Col de la Seigne.

Perhaps this wasn't entirely unexpected. In 2005, despite never having trained on the course, Olmo had finished third at UTMB. And in 2006, his wife Renata, who had missed the race the year before, was there to encourage him. She met him at the finish with a small bag of toiletries so he could take a shower. They had no hotel reservation that night, though, and slept in their car.

Olmo went on to win UTMB again in 2007, becoming, at age fifty-eight, the oldest person ever to win the the race. Today, at age seventy-four, he still runs. The day we talked, he was headed out for a 13-kilometer run with about 400 meters of climbing. "I start on roads, then turn onto small trails. I like to run early in the morning when the roads are quiet.

"I'll keep running," he said, "as long as I'm able."

CORRINE MALCOLM:
"A PILGRIMAGE TO THE MECCA OF TRAIL AND ULTRA"

As one of the central commentators for the UTMB World Series, Corrine Malcolm is known to millions of viewers of the UTMB races around the world. As she sees trail running develop, however, she is also concerned about the growing pains and rectifying inequalities. Before rising to prominence announcing UTMB and other top races, Corrine was both a coach and pro trail runner, eager to get to Chamonix for the race—and also to load up on French pastries!

I came over for the first time in 2018 because I really wanted to be a part of the experience. I just knew it was important. As an unsponsored athlete, I could barely afford to be there, but I shared a house to save money and lived on baguettes and salted butter for a month while I was training on the course and getting to know the valley. I instantly loved the fun and chaotic European race vibe: fast starts, lots of people, elbows everywhere, and a six minute per mile opening pace for no reason.

That same year, the UTMB media team invited me for an interview and to do a little bit of commentary. I guess you could say I'm their worst mistake, because after that they couldn't get rid of me. My involvement snowballed. Being part of the coverage makes for a really fun, busy week. During the live commentating, I become a multi-tasking queen, monitoring the YouTube chat, pulling historical data, getting WhatsApp text updates from friends on the course. I bounce between what feels like 17 different screens, while trying to form a coherent sentence. It's frenetic, but we have great teamwork and I love getting the information back out to viewers.

The coverage, just like the event, is definitely growing and evolving each year. UTMB feels like the world's biggest stage for ultra trail runners. As an elite runner, it feels like you're coming over here to prove yourself and show that you can hang in one of the toughest fields in the world. Even before

I was sponsored, it felt like I needed to figure out a way to get here and show that I could step up into this next level of racing.

Regardless of whether you're an elite, an average runner, or not even running in the race, during all the hype and excitement of the week, it just feels really good to be here. It's like a pilgrimage to the mecca of trail and ultra.

But with UTMB becoming such a big stage and leading the growth and professionalization of the sport, there is also an opportunity, and responsibility, to push the experience in positive ways for all.

One of my biggest worries is the added barrier of entry with the cost of the series and needing to travel all over the world to get UTMB's Running Stones (see graphic page 123). It ends up being a form of economic discrimination.

Creating opportunities for women is another big issue. Female representation at UTMB remains, at best, around 11%, which is low for our sport. There has been confusion about the pregnancy deferral as well as extreme frustration over the Quartz medical rules [which have since been abandoned].

I don't envy the UTMB organization trying to figure out some of these rapid growing pains, but it is necessary. I know it's going to take time, and our community is ready and pushing these issues from the inside. UTMB could lead here. I hope they will come to the table with a plan to make all runners feel welcome and included.

DAVID LANEY: "I CAN'T GET CAUGHT UP IN THE INSANITY"

David Laney is part of the small group of US men to crack the top five at UTMB, finishing 3rd in 2015 and 4th in 2016. Beyond his talent and determination, David became a passionate student of the UTMB course, coming to understand exactly how best to approach the loop.

To begin, slow down. People go stupidly fast at the start. It's basically a road race for the first 15K and will feel easy. You'll convince yourself you won't pay for it later, because it's flat pavement or soft trail with little rollers, but you will. For me, to finish in the top 10, I can't get caught up in the insanity. I have to be in 100th place at 20K.

Coming into the towns is another time people get excited and you'll need to keep cool. Like on the descent into Courmayeur—people will fly by you. I've had 20 people pass me on that descent. You're going to feel horrible as it happens, but try to remember it's a long game and just focus on not rolling an ankle.

You'll probably pass them at the aid station, anyway. I've come into Courmayeur in 30th place and as I head out they say, "You're in 9th!" Wait, I passed 21 people at the aid station? "Yea, they're all sitting on cots, quads burnt." I'm not rushing through the aid stations, either. I try never to feel rushed the entire race. This should be a long, beautiful stroll—you just can't stop.

In fact, until Courmayeur, you don't want to expend any real effort. It should be 100% easy up until then. If it's not easy, hike. If the descent is too hard, walk. I learned this from an old mountain man I met on the trail above Courmayeur. He appeared like an Italian phantom and said, "You do not hit the gas at Courmayeur... You hit the gas at Col Ferret!" Turns out he was right.

The course has two distinct sections— before Col Ferret and after. If you take significant risks or make mistakes in the first half, the consequences are massive. But after Col Ferret, it's time to get in the zone. Not to mention the long runnable descent into Switzerland is where you can finally take the brakes off and fly.

With about 50K to go, around Champex-Lac, you'll hit three final, raging climbs. People are screaming in pain, it's likely hot, and just the worst ever. You want to die, but for me, that's when I start running as hard as I absolutely can.

Both in 2015 and 2016, I had intense experiences in that last section. I found a mental space of complete focus where pain was transformed into something primal. I take the discomfort and channel it into pure energy. It's a feedback loop. It's a sort of nuclear fusion, where energy becomes more energy, exponentially. This has rarely happened to me outside of UTMB. I think this place inspires another level. You let it wash over you and it's super energizing. You become part of a culture that values doing something unique and difficult.

The finish is bittersweet. After this intense experience, mostly alone, you come into town with thousands of people screaming. It feels like being dropped back into reality and is overwhelming, at least for my personality. I just want to get out of there. If someone whispered, "Oh, there's a special second loop, open invitation. Are you in?" My answer would be, "absolutely."

When people ask me to explain UTMB, I deflect, I refuse to answer—because it's unexplainable. There's nothing I can say that will capture it. Instead, I just say, "You should totally go to Chamonix sometime." You don't even need to race, just go experience the place and culture. The trail, Tour de Mont-Blanc, has a magic and a spirit all its own.

COURTNEY DAUWALTER: "OH, I COULD TRY SOMETHING HARD"

After having UTMB in mind for years, Courtney Dauwalter ran the race for the first time in 2019 and took first place among women. In 2021, she came back and set the course record, coming in 7th overall with a time of 22:30:55. Here, she shares her thoughts on why UTMB holds such a special place in the trail running community and some of her most memorable moments.

UTMB came on my radar years before I actually went and did it. I got super into following the coverage online, tracking the names of runners who my husband Kevin and I know. I got to see how cool it looked out there—the glaciers, Mont Blanc, trail running in three countries. I spent three summers in a row tracking UTMB, getting more and more curious each time I watched. Finally I thought to myself, "I gotta get my feet on that course and see if I can even get around that loop!"

What makes UTMB unique is the cool mixture of all the things that make ultra running special. You get that solo vision quest in the dark, when you're running through Italy, picking your way through a boulder field in complete silence. Then you get to roll into Courmayeur or any one of the dozen other towns and soak up the excitement of an insane party.

One of my favorite spots on the course is Notre Dame de la Gorge. You're starting the climb up towards Col du Bonhomme and there are people lining the start of the climb, cheering you on. They create this long tunnel of people, and their only reason for being there is to cheer on us runners as we head out into the night. It's a great big send-off into the mountains.

Both times I have raced UTMB, I really pushed hard on the last climb from up Col des Montets. It stands out for me. You can taste the finish line, but you're not there yet, and there's so much work left to get there. Both years I know I looked like a zombie. I felt like I was moving really slowly and like I had never run before in my life. I was tripping over everything. I was fully in the very back corner of the pain cave! All I could think about was the next step.

UTMB has made more people aware that ultrarunning is a sport. Plus, it's gotten people thinking that just maybe, it's something they can try. To have someone start dreaming and scheming of running a hundred miles when maybe eight years ago they didn't run at all or thought it was impossible, well, that's pretty cool. Getting more people thinking, "Oh, I could try something hard" and seeing more people getting out on the trails, I think all of that is positive.

AN ODE TO TRAIL RUNNING

UTMB 2017 got off to an inauspicious start. Earlier on race day, officials huddled with Chamonix meteorologist Yan Guiezendanner, a past employee of Meteo France. A storm bringing winter conditions was bearing down on the Mont Blanc region. At 11:28 a.m., race organizers texted runners, warning them to be ready for as much as 10 centimeters of snow on the high cols, with temperatures dipping down to −9 degrees Celsius, or 16 degrees Fahrenheit. Visibility would be very reduced, and the race was planning to add additional course markings.

Runners were advised to bring full cold-weather gear, including warmer shoes, gloves, hats, additional layers, and a winter jacket. The text closed with ominous instructions: "Do not stop at high points. Keep moving."

The start was delayed by thirty minutes, and two short course modifications were made to help runners complete the loop.

But as expected, as 6:30 p.m. neared, under overcast skies, Place du Triangle de l'Amitié began to fill with thousands of runners. Some had thousand-yard stares. Others joked about the conditions, trying to ease the anxiety. Almost everyone performed last-minute pre-race rituals of some kind.

I know this, because I was there, one of the 2,537 runners who lined up for the start.

For those of us wearing bib numbers, it was one of the most important moments in our lives. Tears welled in the eyes of many runners, myself included. You have worked for years to qualify, been selected in a lottery, trained at all hours of the day and night, then found a path through the exigencies of work and family life and have funded the cost of getting yourself to Chamonix. And in your heart, you know a simple truth: it may not happen again. In fact, it probably won't.

It is a truism that runners live what feels like a year of their life during a long ultra. One experiences nearly every human emotion, with overdoses of despair and hope, wonderment and suffering. For me, UTMB 2017 did not disappoint in that regard. Twenty-one hours in, as I neared the Italian border with Switzerland, the forecasted tempest bore down on us. At the Arnouva aid station, race officials warned us that conditions ahead would be severe. A few kilometers later, past Refugio Elena at the base of Grand Col Ferret, I looked up to see a thick mantle of dark clouds and blowing snow. I stopped to eat two energy gels and donned every article of clothing I had in my twelve-liter trail-running vest.

Instinctively, runners grouped together. My peloton moved upward into a meteorological melee. Ice pellets froze my eyelids shut and I put gloved fingers to one eyelid after the other so I could see. Minutes from the top of the Col, our group entered a whiteout. I flashed back to my years of winter mountaineering and found myself saying out loud, "You got this, Mayer. You got this." The words were lost to the gale, but the act of self-confidence powered me to the top.

I stumbled to the emergency aid station, kitted out with a large mountaineering tent and staffed by experienced rescuers. One of them, dressed head to toe in a down suit and wearing goggles, bear-hugged me.

It was one of Chamonix's most popular trail runners, Federico Gilardi (see page 51), then the president of the CMBM trail running club.

"Doog!" he yelled, using the French pronunciation of my name, "Keep moving! It will get better!"

Ultras like UTMB are about as pure a test of resilience as one can find. The race, with its many climbs and big-mountain weather, takes every runner and puts him or her into a crucible. It is the hero's journey, sped up: launched into the unknown, we face challenges and hit physical and mental walls, one after the other. If we push through, it can be transformational. One can leave Friday and return to the finish line Sunday, changed forever through suffering and elation, dumbfounded and at a loss for words to explain what just happened. Add in the local support of the eighteen towns en route, the drama of a carefully choreographed event, and some of the world's most striking mountain terrain, and it is not an overstatement to say that UTMB can be life-changing.

A SOUL SPORT

The communal, muscle-powered suffering, the adventuring in the wilds, the desire to plumb the depths, pushing boundaries and growing as a person, the craving to take in sights nature makes available only for those who accept the challenge... These things give trail running its emotional core.

Taken together, they put trail running firmly in the family of soul sports like surfing and climbing. More than a way to burn calories, soul sports are emotionally rich and become part of one's DNA. Some go so far as to call trail running a religion. But whatever nomenclature you attach to it, it is that depth of caring that builds a fierce and loyal community.

Michel Poletti knows this. Catherine does, as well. She has been deeply involved in the trail-running culture for decades, accompanying and supporting Michel as he runs at events around the world, from his solo effort around Mont Blanc in the 1990s to the UTMB World Series races of today. But her own personal history, about which she rarely speaks publicly, prevents her from anything more than light exercise. After David's birth, she began suffering serious hip pain. In 1996, she underwent major pelvic girdle reconstructive surgery that included, in part, a full hip replacement. The operation was successful, but one consequence was the loss of sports she had enjoyed, including alpine and Nordic skiing.

The original group of nine trail runners who met at the Hotel Faucigny in 2002 all had in their DNA a thirst for mountain adventure. UTMB was born with the spirit of the mountains, and that core set of values were baked in from the first day. As a friend once told me, "Stoke is eternal." But is that still true when a business founded by a handful of passionate volunteers becomes an international corporation with dozens of employees, hundreds of thousands of participants, and races around the globe?

BUT IS THERE ROOM FOR IT ALL?

While writing this book, I have been told that UTMB was destroying trail running. That it was bad for the sport, perhaps the worst thing that could have possibly happened. UTMB was pulling trail running to a dark place inhabited by capitalists and egomaniacs with secret Swiss bank accounts. With Ironman in it, trail running as we knew it was done for.

The argument I heard usually went something like this: UTMB's growth and development comes at the expense of the soul of the sport. This is zero-sum math, which assumes that the trail-running community cannot peacefully coexist with a profit-driven race at its pinnacle. It also implies that trail runners cannot make their own choices about where they want to be, come the close of August each year. "People are fearful of the Ironmanification of trail running," said Topher Gaylord, one of the many people I spoke to who think UTMB has been good for the sport. "But I think it's a false narrative. If you really look at it, they're just trying to do the same thing that any great race organizer does, which is create a cool, transformative experience, make sure everyone can get through it safely, and [have] people leave with a deeper appreciation of the local area."

Dave Beeche, the eager trail runner who brought the sport to Ironman's attention, puts it this way: "I think the notion of hanging on to 'what trail running was' is misplaced. Every sport evolves and changes. To me, the exciting thing about trail running is that it's growing. There are big pinnacle events and there will always be a place for community races that cost fifty bucks to enter." That's not to say the change is going to be easy. "There's going to be some rub; that's where you get creative tension. There are going to be fights around the table. It's healthy."

Surfing and climbing are two examples of soul sports that are farther along in their evolution. Both are now Olympic sports. They have grown up and fragmented into niches, but are healthy nonetheless. Will trail running follow the same path? Andy Anderson, with one foot firmly in each world, thinks so. A longtime U.S. National Park Service Climbing Ranger from Colorado's Rockies to Washington's Mount Rainier to Wyoming's Tetons, Anderson also holds a number of Fastest Known Time records, including besting Kilian Jornet's record on a round trip up the Grand Teton. (Anderson did the out-and-back run in 2 hours, 53 minutes and 2 seconds, topping Jornet by a razor-thin 59 seconds.)

"Running started as a mode of transport. More recently it became a form of exercise, and now it's a way to explore the world—but it's all still putting one foot in front of the other," said Anderson. "Runners are starting to specialize, but I don't think it dilutes the experience. There's room for everyone." And there's lots of crossover, too. At home in Truckee, California, Anderson's routine is a case in point. He often runs with two friends who were collegiate running and track stars. "We may have different expertises, but we still love running. Running creates the bond."

As has happened with other soul sports, as trail running grows, so too does the tent. "It's up to the person. Some people will feel more welcome and excited in a race you need to qualify for, and feel part of that community, where there's excitement and music," Kilian Jornet told me, clearly referencing the UTMB experience. "The good thing about running that should never be lost, is that it's diverse. You can have a race like UTMB and Hardrock or a Kima or a Zegama. There are a lot of differences, and that's good."

Topher Gaylord and Kilian Jornet agree, it seems. "There's a place for bigger high-quality, well run, very safe races in the world. I also think there's plenty of space for small grassrootsy community races. There's sort of a debate that's really a non-debate for me. There's room for all of it," Gaylord concludes.

THE CRITICS RUSH IN

Why has trail running's most famous race engendered such strong resistance from trail runners over the years? In any soul sport, each move is closely scrutinized. Everyone in trail running's loyal community is eager to defend the values they see exemplified in the sport. And so, we each become self-appointed arbiters.

To fan the flames, we live in a supercharged, polarized time in history, where listening and giving the benefit of the doubt feels like a lost art. Empathy is in short supply, but there is plenty of righteous indignation to go around.

And UTMB is pushing trail running. In the process, and arguably too often, it makes mistakes (see chapter 4). It's a perfect storm that feeds a sense of indignation and ill will, in lieu of discussion and greater understanding.

Take, for example, access to the Chamonix races for elite runners. Before 2022, the world's best simply had to have a certain race index rating which—to oversimplify a complex equation—broadly equated to an overall ranking in the world of trail racing. Score high enough, and a free entry was yours. As a result, the race had one of the most competitive starting fields in the world.

Starting in 2022, however, with the announcement of dozens of new World Series races with annual championships in Chamonix, everything shifted. Now, runners who want to skip the lottery need to have finished in the top three of a World Series race or in the top ten of the more competitive UTMB World Series Majors races in the fifteen months prior to UTMB Mont Blanc.

This is smart for business, leveraging a coveted starting place in Chamonix to get big-name runners out to races that might seem less glamorous. As Tim Tollefson puts it, "Why not control all of the tributaries into your golden pond?"

Gil Caillet-Bois is the race director of Champéry, Switzerland's Dents-du-Midi race, which is not associated with the UTMB Series. Now well into its fifties, "DDM" is the oldest trail race in the Alps. "UTMB representatives have put forward a desire for openness and inclusion. But most participants, including elite runners, made it clear that the situation is quite

different: if you want to run UTMB, you have to run on the 'By UTMB' circuit, at the expense of other races," he said. "For some, it becomes economically problematic, since you have to travel to one of the qualifying races just to get a chance via UTMB's lottery. For a lot of runners, those races are not nearby and require traveling, often internationally."

Other elite runners with whom I spoke off the record, were also disillusioned. Now these runners need to plan their year around not just one UTMB ultra but at least two. Effectively, it means a major part of their season is devoted to UTMB. Tollefson sees the field getting diluted. "What I have loved about UTMB is that it unofficially served as the World Championship of trail running. A sea of the best-ranked trail runners could converge in Chamonix at the end of every August to duke it out."

SHARING THE LOVE

If you love something, you become an advocate for it. You want others to see what you see, feel what you feel, experience what you have experienced.

Every trail runner I interviewed for this book who had run UTMB said that they still feel that same passion when running the race. Away from the business deals, away from the banners and branding and the crush of the crowds and cameras, anyone who runs UTMB still feels some of that magic. Strip away the artifice, and what remains is one of the world's best courses and two of the most experienced race organizers anywhere. There is still plenty of love for UTMB.

Trail running continues to grow, and rapidly. And no one shares trail running with more people around the world than UTMB. To find evidence of this, you need look no further than the search bar on your browser. Each August, at the end of the month, Google searches for the term "Ultra Running" more than triple, according to an internal Google search-trend study from a major trail running shoe brand. UTMB brings people to trail running. I haven't done all the UTMB races, but I have run and finished UTMB, CCC and MCC twice, and TDS once. And each time, friends and family around the globe have been able to tune in to follow my progress.

Whether you run UTMB or not, think Chamonix is a circus or find yourself addicted to the Sommet Mondial du Trail, UTMB has brought trail running to the world. The race is, simply, everywhere—and in recent years has spread to one of the biggest trail running areas in the world, China. "The Chinese consider UTMB as the ultimate target of their own trail running career," said Fu-Zhao Xiang, a Chinese trail runner and one of the world's best. She has run UTMB three times, finishing as high as 7th. "It's the Olympics of trail running," she wrote to me via an interpreter. "I want to run UTMB every year." That global reach has exposed a new generation of trail runners to the sport. It's simply impossible not to view the race as a central factor in trail running's growth.

Take, for example, Mike Ambrose, who grew up in southern New Jersey, and didn't so much as see a mountain until he was eighteen. Living in downtown Philadelphia after college, Ambrose didn't know much about trail running. Surfing YouTube one day, he came across a Salomon video about UTMB. "It totally captivated me. I was hooked," Ambrose said. "I heard American runners talk about why they liked the race. I saw Kilian for the first time. I connected my own running to what they were saying, and I totally fell in love with it: Mont Blanc, the crowds, the scenery, and the most wonderful, joyful, collective experience of running I had ever seen. Even the back of the pack had the same great spirit." Ambrose bought a pair of Salomon trail running shoes. "I would take the bus across town and run trails, pretending I was in Chamonix."

It didn't stop there. Ambrose quit his job, moved to Colorado, and started working at a trail-running shop in Breckenridge. Three years later, he was running through the streets of Chamonix, working in nearby Annecy at Salomon's world headquarters. He went on to develop one of the brand's most popular trail-running shoes ever, the Ultraglide, and today is USA Country Manager for Kilian Jornet's new company, NNormal. "Without UTMB," said Mike, "I'm not sure I would have ever gone down this path. It's the spirit that caught my attention and made it special for me."

Ambrose, by the way, has more than returned the favor to his sport. He spent a year traveling the US nearly every week, teaching "How to Trail Run" workshops for Salomon across the country.

Certainly, his story is exceptional. But for every Mike Ambrose, there are hundreds of others who have been inspired enough by UTMB to Google "trail running," and soon put on a pair of shoes and seek out a trail. "What UTMB has done is provide this experience to more people," Topher Gaylord said. "In a way, it's the most inclusive race in the world."

Who can argue against more people getting away from screens and out into the natural world to challenge themselves?

"WITH GREAT POWER COMES GREAT RESPONSIBILITY"

Dylan Bowman is a keen observer of the path UTMB is on. "I take Catherine and Michel at their word that the spirit of trail running remains their North Star," he said. "They get the sport, and Michel represents the beating heart of trail running. But I don't know that they've done that much to cultivate the spirit." Bowman's suggestions? "They could have a softer edge. Do a little more outreach, a little more giving back, and open up a bit more about the conversations they're having and the decisions they're making."

Bowman is spot on. It's a change that would benefit both UTMB and the wider sport. But it requires a cultural shift toward greater openness and communication, toward engagement prior to decision making.

Other races around the world are leading the sport forward ethically, environmentally, and socially. Races of all sizes are working every day to make trail running more inclusive, more representative of society at large. In doing so, they make it more welcoming and lay the base for an even stronger future.

UTMB has done good work through its nonprofit association. But it could do much more. The push for gender parity provides an illuminating example. "There are gender norms that hold women back," Stephanie Case notes. "Who's still responsible for kids, for the family? Women. There is this notion that training is selfish, too. That comes up a lot more for women than men." Case points out that adding in qualifying races only exacerbates the problem for women. "UTMB is so prominent. They have a huge opportunity to lead the world of trail running and they have failed," said Case. "They're setting us all back by not taking those steps."

Even Colorado's Hardrock 100, a race that has been criticized for its "old-boy" style of operation, is getting in on the action. Despite their reputation—or perhaps because of it—the board of directors has made a conscious decision to consider new ideas. They have created a volunteer equity committee to address the low number of women taking part in the race. They have also hosted panels and discussion groups to address gender equity. Case, who finished second in Hardrock in 2022, served on the committee and knows something about promoting inclusivity. A human-rights lawyer for the United Nations, she started the international nonprofit Free to Run, which enables women and girls in conflict areas to run safely. The Hardrock 100 board announced its new policy in July 2021, and at the start line on July 15, 2022, the race had its highest number of women participants ever.

High Lonesome, a 100-mile trail race through Colorado's Rocky Mountains, provides another example. The race now splits entrants into two lotteries, one for men and a second for women, assuring a 50:50 gender balance at the start line. In previous years, about 20% of the runners at the start line were women. "We believe that this imbalance had a negative impact on our sport, and specifically our race's community," the organizers wrote in a gender-equity policy released at the end of 2021.

The 100-mile Western States Endurance Run based in Auburn, California, is another major race that is finding a path forward. In 2019, they adopted a podium policy for transgender runners. "Western States has gotten out front of the issue," former Runners World editor Amby Burfoot announced in a New York Times article three months later. "Western States is at the forefront of policies like gender inclusion."

None of these races tackle complex issues with closed meetings of their founders. Western States is illustrative. It has a fifteen-member board of directors that makes for a wide range of input when considering sensitive topics.

On the specific questions of gender balance and welcoming transgender athletes, Michel Poletti said, "We are working on it. We have a responsibility to have clear and inclusive rules." Still, UTMB remains behind many of the world's great trail races when it comes to inclusivity. While a privately held company is not obligated to be out front on these issues, the race nonetheless loses credibility and standing with many trail runners if it cedes that high ground. "You will see us putting these policies in place," Michel Poletti said. "I just ask for some patience."

Stephanie Case has a nearly perfect visual for the choice facing UTMB and other major events like it. "You can either be a mirror of what you are seeing in the sport, or you can be a door. If you're a mirror, you're

just reflecting back the inequality that already exists. If you're a door, you can be a leader. You can lead everyone to a better place."

Trail runners themselves also have power. "As the sport moves into this next generation, toward which UTMB is leading us, it's incumbent upon us as fans of the sport and participants in their races to ensure that UTMB maintains the spirit," said Bowman.

UTMB CODA, 2017

The drama of my 2017 UTMB didn't end at Grand Col Ferret. Far from it. Two hours later, my race got much worse. I sprained my ankle on entirely uninteresting terrain. At the Champex-Lac aid station, I huddled in the corner of the enormous tent, shivering violently as darkness descended and rain fell. The temperature was falling, and it was perfect weather for a bad case of hypothermia.

Out of ideas, exhausted and paralyzed with indecision, I clumsily speed-dialed my most trusted source of trail wisdom, Alistair Bignell. A trail-running guide with years of experience, Al had top finishes at several of the UTMB series races under his belt. I could always count on him to be both sensible and inspirational.

"I think I need to drop," I said.

"Before you do anything, go see one of the docs."

Al gave a brief pep talk, and then I stumbled into a heated medical tent. Twenty minutes later, I was warmed up and sported a professionally taped ankle. The French doctor was matter-of-fact: "Allez, go to Chamonix!" And at exactly 10 pm, I stepped cautiously out of the tent and headlong into one of the hardest challenges of my life.

For the next 14 hours, I half-ran, half-hobbled my way through 45 kilometers of mountainous terrain. During the course of what became a bitter grudge match against the trail, 205 runners passed me. Perhaps thanks to a final burst of adrenaline, I ran the final few hundred meters to the finish line. I had been on the course for 42:11:18 and finished 1,059th of the 1,687 finishers who made it back to Chamonix that year.

I might have felt like it, but I was not the last official runner. That year's Lanterne Rouge honor fell to Emil Duch, with a time of 46:15:23. Duch, from Warsaw, Poland, struggled at the end of the race, suffering from difficulty breathing and a swollen foot. After two nights without sleep, he was hallucinating. "I was smiling," he says, "but I felt pain inside."

Duch realized something was up when two race officials started following him. They were, they said, a "live finish line. If we overtake you, you're out!" At the actual finish line, the crowd started singing and clapping. After Duch finished, someone approached him and said something in French. A friend translated. He was going on stage with the winners. "I was so tired I didn't even analyze it. I saw hundreds of people applauding me. Someone on the PA announced something, and another runner took my hand. Only later did I realize it was François D'Haene, the winner," Duch told me. "When I finally sat down and drank something, I smiled inside. One guy who passed by asked if he could take a picture with me. It was funny for me, but very nice."

After the ceremony, Duch and his friends packed up their car and drove 1,600 kilometers back to Warsaw. Duch slept the entire way. "When I got home, every muscle ached, but I felt fulfilled." A few days later, Duch was scrolling through Facebook when he saw a photo of himself on stage. "Look, he's from our country!" someone had commented. "I received many congratulations," said Duch. "I felt like a winner."

A NEW GENERATION

For many years now, Michel Poletti has been a steady, strong ultra runner. On Friday, August 26, 2022, at age sixty-seven, he lined up for the start of his seventh UTMB. His finish time of 41:57:48 placed him second of just six finishers in his age category. He finished 1,129th of 1,789 overall. There were just eight runners older than he was.

How much longer can he run a hundred miles around Mont Blanc? "For the moment, I'm fast enough to not be fighting against the time barriers," he said. But it's not easy to continue to run, he admits. "I have some trouble with my knees and my back. Maybe another ten years?" Poletti has a new goal in sight, too: to beat the time of the oldest runner ever to complete UTMB. He has some tough competition. In 2009, the Swiss runner Werner Schweizer, then age seventy, finished the race in 34:07:29, placing 227th out of 1,383 runners.

For the last two decades, UTMB has been in the hands of Catherine and Michel Poletti. From that first lineup on a stormy pre-dawn morning in August 2003 through to the drama-filled weeks of races beamed around the world in more recent years, the race has been a manifestation of their strengths and weaknesses, their hopes and dreams, their ambition and ego, and, yes, their idiosyncrasies.

And now, as the Polettis promised Ironman, the family business is being passed to their son and daughter, David and Isabelle. It does not seem a burden to the two siblings. They are eager successors; both have been active in UTMB since the early days.

While studying information technology with her future husband, Mickaël, Isabelle Viseux Poletti built the very first UTMB website. To track runners around Mont Blanc, the two developed what later became LiveTrail, a sophisticated trail-running tracking system that combines runner data with terrain models to develop estimated arrival times at key points along a race course. As LiveTrail developed, the company licensed its services to other races, and today is used by 156 events and 717 races all around the world. It has become a way for participants' families and friends to engage with the races, wherever they take place.

Starting in 2021, "Isa" transitioned to a new role, Race Director for UTMB Mont-Blanc, and manager of the UTMB races in the rest of France. She is now responsible for relationships with the eighteen towns through which UTMB races pass. She also manages the UTMB Mont-Blanc staff and coordinates UTMB with the World Series events.

She lives in Chamonix with Mickaël and their three kids. Sports are in her blood. At age nineteen, she was on the French national biathlon team and finished tenth in the world in the junior women's category. She was also a member of France's women's biathlon relay team, which finished fourth.

David is a true UTMB child, celebrating a birthday each year on August 29th, usually during the race. At the first edition, sixteen-year-old David was a volunteer, building signs, handing out race bibs, and working at aid stations. In later years, he worked at the race's nerve center, the Poste de Commandement de la Course, or "PC Course," then located in the mayor's offices. He has run UTMB twice, in 2007 and 2008. in 2008, he would have finished third in his age group, had it not been for a runner his age who won the overall race—a runner whose last name was Jornet.

David has an educational and career background in communications technology. He joined LiveTrail in 2012, where he started out working in marketing. Today he is the company's executive director and oversees a staff of six.

At age six, David started Nordic skiing with his father. The two used trail running to train for skiing—a training regime that eventually got flipped on its head. The summer before the first edition of UTMB, at age fifteen, he ran the 23-kilometer Cross du Mont-Blanc. After a break to start a family, he's now running regularly again. At the moment, he doesn't have the time to train for ultras and limits his racing distance to 50 kilometers. He and his wife Estelle have two kids.

What is life like, with UTMB all in the family? Isabelle sees both sides of the coin. "UTMB takes up a lot of space in our lives and at times it feels too much," she said. "But we are lucky: it keeps us together as a family and we always have plenty to talk about at family get-togethers." Isabelle might count herself lucky to have David as a brother. "The most important thing in keeping our relationships healthy is to forget one's ego," David told me. "In my case, this means not being bothered by having my big sister as a boss!"

THE RUN DOWN

It is mid-November, and I am trail running the final 10 kilometers of the UTMB course. Just for fun. Winter is descending from on high. A few hundred meters above me, at Flégère, a thin blanket of snow coats the alpine terrain. Soon, these trails will be buried in drifts and swept by avalanches. At home, a quiver of trail running shoes will be stowed away for the season. Skiers will arrive from all over the world.

It's a poignant time of year. The season is ending, and I am greedy for a final run. My labradoodle, Izzy, bounces forward, reveling in the joys of moving fast along a trail. I do too. My brain is on meditative autopilot, my feet are dancing from rock to soil to leaves to rock.

I stop for a moment at Chalet Floria, a rustic mountain café where, in summer, the staff would be busy serving tarte aux myrtilles and café au lait to hikers and trail runners. The chalet's windows are boarded up against the storms to come. No one is here. I imagine Kilian and Katie, who ninety-one days earlier ran this same path, experiencing a few last quiet moments before their life-changing finishes amid tens of thousands of cheering onlookers. I think, too, of the thousands of other runners behind them, ordinary people on the cusp of one of the most extraordinary accomplishments of their lives. My recollections of my own two UTMBs are hazy. Though I only ran about half as fast as Kilian Jornet, I was still in my own pain cave, and not much was getting stored in my mind in the way of memories. But the emotions are etched in my soul: suffering, joy, accomplishment, wonderment, and, yes, a tear or two.

My mind wanders, trying to make sense of the kaleidoscope that is UTMB. No matter what your take on it, the story—from Bachelard to Jornet and all of us in between—is a remarkable one. I think of the richness of the event, the accomplishments of the twin UTMB entities, profit and nonprofit, the business of trail running, the explosive growth, the criticisms and passions, the larger-than-life personalities, the personal race dramas, known and unknown, of all the ordinary runners. In this book I have tried, in my small way, to grasp hold of it all and give it a good look.

I heard so many different sides of the story. I got distraught phone calls and emails and WhatsApp messages from passionate trail running friends and acquaintances who warned me to have nothing to do with UTMB. I spoke to people who love coming to Chamonix in August: eager volunteers; journalists and photographers who are grateful for the attention UTMB has brought to their work; runners who consider it their greatest achievement to have finished UTMB.

I often sensed the challenge for UTMB has been not in the vision, but in the details, in miscommunication, in the unforced errors. I heard from respected trail running insiders and elite athletes, who felt that decisions had been made without hearing from key stakeholders, and those on the margins of trail running, who are nonetheless impacted by UTMB's every move.

The challenge, of course, is that in UTMB, we are getting one version of the values of trail running. And that's not necessarily in sync with what the rest of the world wants. That gap leaves a space where miscommunication and misunderstanding rush in, creating a distrust that benefits no one.

And what I noticed most was there was so much heat, and so little light. Every move by UTMB was scrutinized, but too often it was without the knowledge or background to give an informed opinion. In the world of trail running, the online trolls gravitated to UTMB.

Through all the static, all the passion for trail running turned on its head and focussed on Chamonix, there were smart voices who made constructive, thoughtful points dispassionately. Their views coalesced into one central theme: if they are to lead the world of trail racing, people told me, UTMB needs to be more engaged with stakeholders, not just shareholders. Several people I talked with attribute this to what is commonly known in the business world as "Founders Syndrome." "Founders are great visionaries and excellent at establishing a venture," said Stephanie

Case, who stepped back after founding Free to Run, leaving its management to an executive director. "Having founders managing the company ten years later is not healthy. The roles are different."

John Medinger shares this same concern. One of the most influential forces in ultra-running today, Medinger has been the owner and publisher of *UltraRunning Magazine*, race director of the popular Quad Dipsea race in San Francisco's Bay Area, founder of California's Lake Sonoma 50 and president and board member of the Western States Endurance Run. In his professional life, he was a senior executive at a Fortune 500 company. Founders, he pointed out, need to transition to become executives. "You can still be the visionary, but you need to learn to delegate. Hire good people, empower them, guide them, challenge them, encourage them, set goals for them," he said, outlining the to-do list for a successful leader. "And then get the hell out of the way and let them go to work."

But brands, athletes, organizers, coaches...none of them can just walk away from UTMB. It is the giant in the room. I heard consistently from top runners that this created a tension for those who would rather be somewhere other than Chamonix at the end of August. Because, well, UTMB is the Capitale Mondiale du Trail. Brands insist that their athletes go to Chamonix. And the enormity of the power of UTMB, I found, led to a form of self-censorship among many with whom I spoke. Many had to be coaxed to talk frankly about their feelings. Some refused outright. Others were obviously awkward. Stephanie Case put it succinctly: "Many athletes don't speak out about UTMB because of the power it has." Several high-level people in the trail-running world spoke to me on the condition that our conversations would be off the record—an indication of the clout, real or perceived, of UTMB.

The race is more than just a stand-alone business. At the heart of trail running, I heard from runners, journalists, podcasters, and business folk that UTMB needs more openness, broader input, better communication, and a deeper global perspective to avoid misunderstandings.

And yet, under the layers of deals, beyond the sponsor banners and brands, UTMB is still driven by the emotion of the spectacle. The sheer accomplishment of ordinary and extraordinary runners. Rémi Duchemin, the person who has had the deepest understanding of UTMB finances for a decade now, puts it this way: "Contrary to what some people like to think, UTMB is a company driven by emotions—mainly the emotions we want to generate for runners—and not by numbers."

UTMB. It's all still a work in progress.

Trail running is filled with wonderful quirks, and here, I think, is another. In what other major international sporting event can one of the founders and managers, twenty years in, also toe the line? In all my hours speaking with Catherine and Michel Poletti, one thing was always clear to me: they are both passionate about trail running and care deeply about its future. If they are opinionated, it is from the heart and with thought about the values of the sport. Are they ambitious, and do they want UTMB to stay atop the world of trail racing? Absolutely. But it is not all about the money, as some charge. If it were, both would be nicely retired now, and not living in the home they moved into years ago, sharing a little electric Renault Zoe.

Izzy and I run down Rue Joseph Vallot, and I decide to take the same route as the twenty thousand or so finishers over the past two decades. So, we turn left onto Avenue Michel Croz, run along the Arve river for a moment, and pass the original start and finish next to the statue of Horace Bénédict de Saussure and Jacques Balmat. I follow Balmat's pointing finger to my left and spot the domed, snowy summit of Mont Blanc 10 kilometers and 3,772 meters of vert away. It always seems so close. Finally, we run along Place de l'Église, next to the mayor's office. We cross the finish line and no one cheers for us.

The vagaries of business, a complex web of values, and a host of outside forces—including each of us—will shape UTMB's future. But this much we know: come next August, another 2,500 runners will file into this space, and there will be new stories to tell.

NOTES AND ACKNOWLEDGEMENTS

Trail running is a small world, and conflicts of interest are inevitable. In the interest of disclosure, I am part owner with Martina Valmassoi of the company Insane Inside Design, and own Run the Alps, a trail-running tour company that has partnered with UTMB. In 2018, I did freelance work checking translations for UTMB for a few weeks. I have also worked for Salomon. Hillary Gerardi works part time for Run the Alps. Run the Alps has cooperated in the past with companies that are UTMB sponsors.

This project, and the behind-the-scenes stories herein, would not have been possible without the openness of Catherine and Michel Poletti. I always felt free to ask them anything. Michel and Catherine, your willingness to accept any question made this writer's job much easier and helped me in my goal to craft an honest story. Thank you.

Produced over the course of six very intense months, this project included more than fifty interviews and over 1,000 pages of resulting annotated transcripts. It could not have happened without the hard work of a wonderful team.

My thanks to Matt Abbott, Mike Ambrose, Antoine Aubour, René Bachelard, Dave Beeche, Mathieu Blanchard, Mara Borghesio, Rory Bosio, Robbie Britton, David Callahan, Michel Charlet, Bob Crowley, Ashley Curtis, Vincent Delebarre, Marion Delobel, François D'Haene, Jesse Dubey, Emil Duch, Nicolas Durochat, Laura Font, Eric Fournier, Nicolas Fréret, Aina Garcia, Emily Geldard, Hillary Gerardi, Julien Gilleron, Mathieu Girard, Kilian Jornet, Hugo Joyeux, Meb Keflezighi, Jay Kelley, David Laney, Stephanie Lefferts, Meg Mackenzie, Nico Mermoud, Jasmine Mitchell, Krissy Moehl, Marco Olmo, Fabrice Perrin, Malcolm Pittman, David Poletti, Isabelle Viseux Poletti, Laurence Poletti-Gautier, Katie Schide, Barry Siff, Grace Staberg, Karla Valladares, Fu-Zhao Xiang, and the UTMB staff.

Helvetiq is a wonderful international publisher, with a lively, smart and supportive team. Thank you to everyone there, and especially Hadi Barkat, Alizée Dabert, Aurélie Fourel, Myriam Hériter, Eleni Karametaxas, Raphaël Nicolet, Aude Pidoux, Ewelina Proczko, Tina Stebler, and Ajsa Zdravkovic,

I'm terribly sorry if I forgot someone—the mistake is mine.

I'm grateful to Topher Gaylord, Andy Jones-Wilkins, John Medinger, Brian Metzler, Emily Geldard, Johanna Flashman, Jenn Hughes and Malcolm Pittman for reading TK-filled drafts of the manuscript.

Thanks to Dylan Bowman and the Freetrail podcast.

Johanna Flashman and Jenn Hughes edited the In Their Own Voices passages and drafted the introductions, painstakingly annotated over a thousand pages of interviews, and were always there with wise comments and moral support. In addition, Johanna developed and did the research behind many of the charts, illustrations, and images. This book was a full-on sprint. Thanks for being along for it.

The best thing a writer can have, other than strong coffee and a retina-quality screen, is a wonderful editor. Richard Harvell, thanks for arriving at just the right moment and always nudging me to the next level.

We can both thank Peter Greer for whatever concise, clear sentences exist in these pages.

English Knowles, thanks for being my go-to crew and keeping me moving forward in an ultra that was harder than UTMB, by far.

Hey Izzy, I'm done! Let's go for a run!

INDEX